PALESTINE IN THE ARAB DILEMMA

PALESTINE IN
THE ARAB DILEMMA

WALID W. KAZZIHA

CROOM HELM LONDON

BARNES & NOBLE BOOKS · NEW YORK
(a division of Harper & Row Publishers, Inc.)

© 1979 Walid W. Kazziha
Croom Helm Ltd, 2-10 St John's Road, London SW11

British Library Cataloguing in Publication Data

Kazziha, Walid W
    Palestine in the Arab dilemma.
    1. Fedayeen   2. Arab countries — Foreign relations
    I. Title
    332.4'2'095694   DS119.7

    ISBN 0-85664-864-7

Published in the USA 1979 by
HARPER & ROW PUBLISHERS, INC.
BARNES & NOBLE IMPORT DIVISION

Library of Congress Cataloging in Publication Data

Kazziha, Walid.
    Palestine in the Arab dilemma.
    Includes bibliographical references and index.
    1. Palestinian Arabs — Politics and government —
Addresses, essays, lectures. 2. Arab countries —
Politics and government — 1945 —   Addresses, essays,
lectures.   3. Jewish-Arab relations — Addresses, essays,
lectures.   I. Title.
DS119.7.K37   320.9'17'4927   78-10543
ISBN 0-06-494004-7

This book is part of a series of works which the Istituto Affari Internazionali is publishing within the framework of a research programme financed by the Ford Foundation dedicated to the problems of the Mediterranean.

Printed in Great Britain by
Billing & Sons Limited, Guildford, London and Worcester

CONTENTS

FOREWORD

The Arab-Israeli war — like all wars — is a great 'simplifier'. It creates the simplistic impression that there are two opposing fronts, each one united and firmly single minded in its hostility towards the other, with well defined objectives and a clear-cut conception of what it wants from victory. Of course, this is not the case. Not only are there large and ever growing political differences inside Israel, but the difficulties on the Arab side are just as plentiful and as serious. The war is breaking up into a series of micro-conflicts, both within the two camps and between the Arabs and Israelis. A better grasp of these conflicts is the key to an attempt at understanding the war itself and, perhaps, to putting an end to it.

The most notorious of these micro-conflicts — and at the same time the one most frequently ignored — is between the Arabs and the Palestinians. This has been through some very 'hot' phases, ranging from the Black September in Jordan to the Lebanese civil war; from the creation of the 'Rejection' Front to the various terrorist actions by the Palestinian organisations (which, while certainly aimed at hitting Israel and her real or supposed allies, were also intended to support one or other of the factions in the Arab-Palestinian conflict). There is a complex scenario to this conflict, with component parts of varying importance, such as: the development of the Arab-Israeli war; the internal policies of the various Arab countries and regimes; the international policy and military alliances of the Arab states; and the internal policies of, and the reciprocal relations between, the various Palestinian organisations.

There is no history of this conflict, nor any clear methodological definition of the protagonists and the relationships between them. On the contrary, its very existence is sometimes denied and there is condemnation only of the 'betrayal' by one or other of the Arab political leaders of the cause of Arab-Palestinian unity. For instance, this is the main accusation levelled by the 'Rejection' Front against Sadat at present. However, there is more to it than this.

This book is written by a Lebanese intellectual of Syrian extraction, who was in his day involved in militant organisations and now
lectures at the American University in Cairo. In a previous book (*Revolutionary Transformation in the Arab World; Habash and His Comrades
from Nationalism to Marxism*, Charles Knight, London 1974), he tried
to provide a critical history of the birth of the Palestinian liberation
movement, and at the same time, of the political development of the
revolutionary pan-Arab movement. The problems as put by Kazziha are
fairly classic in their way: What is the correct objective for the Palestinians? Where do their real interests lie? How do these coincide with
those of the various Arab states? He draws a clear-cut conclusion: there
is in fact a clash of interests. The pan-Arab movement and the Palestinians are mutually contradictory, and there is an even greater dis-
crepancy between the Palestinian position and the Arab regimes.
Lastly, there is a contradiction between present Arab policy and the
revolutionary movement. The Palestinians, in his view, are used in turn
as puppets, cannon fodder and barter goods; as the *casus belli* or the
casus foederis: as a pretext for imperialist adventures or aspirations to
hegemony; and as a scapegoat for all manner of policies with which
they have nothing to do. All their actions are turned to the advantage
of one side or the other. Even when they ostensibly win greater bargaining power (as at the Arab summit meeting at Rabat when they were
officially recognised as representing Palestinian interests), the Palestinian organisations have to be prepared for new disasters and be prepared
to provide the justification for fresh 'betrayals'. The fact is (Kazziha
seems to suggest) that it is not so much a matter of 'betrayal' as of a
logical attempt by the stronger regimes to suppress what they see as
a 'disruptive' element, an undisciplined variable in their calculations, a
drifting mine afloat in situations which should be consolidated and
brought under a tight and centralised control.

This, in brief, is the starting point of Kazziha's book. However, it
provides a much fuller development of ideas which are in their way
much more contradictory and complex.

In fact, the whole situation in the Middle East is changing rapidly.
What exactly, at the present moment, is a Middle Eastern 'state'?
Certainly something more than the old 'protectorates' of the colonial
era, but something different again from a European nation-state. Take

Israel for example, with its frontiers as they stand today (including the West Bank), and try to imagine it in ten or twenty years' time, as though a more or less durable 'peace' had come about in the interim. What we would have is a classical example of a Middle Eastern state, with about 55 to 60 per cent of the population being of Jewish origin (of whom about 80 per cent would have been born in Israel and lack any experience of other countries or cultures) and with the rest of the population being of Arab extraction belonging to various different religions or sects. Such a state would have naturally indistinct frontiers, continually crossed by nomadic tribes and a growing system of trade and social links in the border areas. At present, Israel is already establishing colonies – not only for imperialist or 'security' reasons – in territories which she recognises as belonging to other states. In doing so she is only anticipating a trend which will develop naturally on its own in peacetime and which has been a permanent and centuries-old feature of settlements in the Middle East. The difficulties of land cultivation, the importance of grazing for cattle-rearing and the natural affinities of the different peoples were once the motives for large-scale transmigration in this area, and this tendency has continued and increased, due to the Arab-Israeli war, the inter-Arab wars and civil and political conflicts. The oil money added a new dimension to these transmigrations and gave another stir to the melting-pot of cultures, nations and tribes in the Middle East. How can it even be supposed that all this will phase out in peacetime? On the contrary, this trend will certainly become stronger. All the more so if the Palestinians are to gain a measure of recognition and the Arab countries keep up their present drive towards economic development. Today, Palestinians and Egyptians form the vast majority of migrants; tomorrow the Israelis are the most likely candidates. Thus, there is an 'identity' problem in the Middle East which affects all the states without exception and is far more difficult to solve than the presently much-vaunted problem of 'military security' in the border areas. The truth is that there are no frontiers in this area which are not somehow fictitious and even more unreal and hazy than many frontiers in Europe.

The Arab-Israeli war has, therefore, been superimposed on another historical process of much greater breadth and importance: the construction of solid and credible states in the Middle East. There are many possible ways to this end, and almost all of them have already been tried by resourceful local politicians. One way is to aim at building a 'strong regime', either directly or indirectly under military control (initially at least) through a party and an ideology, as in the case of the Syrian and Iraqi Baath, or the FLN in Algeria. Another way, as experimented in Lebanon, is to aim at a 'contractual' type of regime based on the combination, by some kind of alchemy, of the pressures and counter-pressures of various religious communities; some states put their faith in the power of money, or — like Israel — try to base the state on religion and myth. Or, again, a more or less revolutionary and socialist regime can be attempted, or a combination of the different formulae. Nevertheless the fact remains that all these solutions have been attempted, but none has been able, to date, to guarantee the stability, continuity and security these states so much want. Even less so have these policies helped the states to clearly establish and demarcate their national territory.

When the Arab League was set up immediately after the war, the pan-Arab concept was no more than a slogan. Relations between the individual Arab states were limited by their weakness and serious problems of internal organisation. Continual changes of regime (which took place everywhere, to a certain extent, and at a positively dizzy speed in Syria and Iraq), the struggle against colonialism and the problem of getting together even a barely credible military response to Israel, took up practically all the Arabs' energies. Their almost total lack of resources, due to the hold kept by the big multinationals over the oil supplies, prevented them from developing an independent line of their own with any hope of success. This situation was abruptly reversed after 1973, thanks to the increase in oil prices which was made possible by the gradual reappropriation of their oil wealth by the producer countries after the 1967 war. Now, for the first time, there is a real transnational class throughout the Middle East, exercising economic power as well as political and military power. Important working alliances are being formed (for example, Saudi Arabia's links with Egypt and the Sudan) and intricate political operations are being mounted on the basis of the greater freedom of action permitted by the petrodollar system. The Palestinians themselves, financed on this basis, are becoming increasingly a transnational political reality and can no longer be contained in a few restricted areas around Israel.

This new transnational reality has not, as yet, found expression in corresponding international institutions which could control its policy-making, serve as a clearing house and, above all, identify and lay down concrete common objectives to be shared by the new ruling class. In practice what happens is that at the level of the various international bodies (the Arab League, the Arab summit meetings, OPEC and OAPEC sessions, etc.) the national ruling groups work out a series of personal alliances, either between 'likeminded' groups or else with only limited political objectives, according to a complicated system of counter-balances. This explains how the 'moderate' Suadis come to be financing the Palestinians along with the 'revolutionary' Iraqis, while at the same time they are helping Egypt to buy arms and technology from the West. Or again, why the Libyans are financing the regime in Ethiopia but simultaneously backing the Eritrean 'revolutionaries' as well, and so on. Alliances of this type therefore have at least three main faults.

First, they do not reflect a consistent and continuous political strategy and so do not contribute towards a greater degree of internal stability in the Middle East. On the contrary, every time some alliance begins to form which could serve as a point of reference (for instance, the Saudi Arabia-Egypt agreement), the other countries immediately join forces against it.

Second, they are heavily conditioned by the internal political objectives of the different groups, which use such alliances to strengthen their own ever precarious situation on the home front. This is the real motivation behind the Syrian intervention in Lebanon, either on the side of the Maronites or the Palestinians, just as it explains the support of the Palestinians by Saudi Arabia. All this increases the instability of the international situation, which is too much at the mercy of the small degree of solidarity the Arab regimes can muster internally.

They cannot be transformed into permanent institutions with a certain amount of authority. And this prevents an effective redistribution of the oil revenues between the producer and consumer countries inside the Arab world, and accentuates the negative aspects of the political string-pulling associated with bilateral aid.

The Palestinian liberation movement is caught up in the midst of these developments. On the one hand, it benefits from this position; it gets funds, solidarity and international recognition because it is part of this pan-Arab transnational complex. On the other hand it pays for its dependence, and the weaker the transnational system is and the more tightly bound to the individual regimes' internal problems, the greater and more cruel the cost to the Palestinian movement. This is all the more so since the movement still has to define its strategy and its real political objectives.

Some would prefer to interpret it as a purely traditional 'national liberation' movement, fighting to regain its own territory on which to build a nation. This is obviously the best solution for the present Arab regimes; it narrows down the Palestinian objectives to the struggle against Israel and, above all, keeps alive the pretence that the Palestinian settlements in various Arab countries (Syria, Lebanon, Jordan, etc.) are only 'temporary'. These countries can therefore continue to treat the Palestinians like political 'objects' which they do not need to consult or allow for in their internal policy-making.

The trouble with this theory is that it is too abstract. In the first instance, it is obvious that without totally annihilating Israel, the Palestinians could never all return to that area. And as for a 'reduced-scale' solution, such as a Palestinian state consisting of the West Bank and the Gaza Strip, there is absolutely no question of its being a large enough area to contain a much bigger population than the one it is already supporting. There is already a threat of overpopulation given the present growth rate. In the second place, this theory does not clear up the relation between the claim to a Palestinian homeland and the other objectives of the Arab countries. What are the real priorities? On the one hand, it is clear that nobody could legitimately expect to speak 'in the name' of the Palestinians, as from time to time over the last few years Jordan, Syria and Egypt actually have done. But, on the other hand, it is also obvious that the Palestinians cannot expect to subordinate political and military decisions on peace or war to their own interests, without surrendering their autonomy. Since the Arabs do not control the Palestinians and neither do the latter control the Arabs, the situation is ever more ambiguous and results in a series of short-term tactical alliances rapidly followed by equally brief and violent confrontations.

Another school of thought has it that the territorial claims of the Palestinians can have no credibility (and in general, that the Palestinians cannot hope to impose their objectives) unless there is a change in the Arab political scene. This is precisely Walid Kazziha's point. Those who accept this view therefore accept the definition of the Palestinians as a 'drifting mine', or, to put it another way, as the 'structural contradiction' within the Arab world. In this case, the victory of the Palestinian cause would necessitate not only the defeat of Israel but also (and probably *first of all*) the overthrow of the present Arab regimes. Only in this way, in fact, could it be hoped to create an effective 'pan-Arab' policy on a Middle East scale, capable of reabsorbing the Palestinians, keeping the conflict under control and producing comprehensive solutions which would also allow for the present-day Israeli nation. Then, the question of a Palestinian 'territory' or 'homeland' would cease to be important, or would be viewed at most as a question of tactics to speed up the general process of change. Obviously, the second theory is perceived as a threat by the Arab regimes and therefore clashes head-on with the present political and military management of Middle Eastern affairs.

In a sense, thus, both these strategies contain real assessments and correct analyses, but both turn out to be politically non-viable and therefore unsuccessful. The truth is that the 'national' solution (the Palestinian homeland) has come up at a moment when throughout the Third World it has become only too clear how weak national structures are and how dangerous they can be to the maintenance of relative stability and peace; while conversely the 'revolutionary' solution would involve a consensus of national Arab political forces and Palestinian forces on a joint project which at present does not even exist.

Sadat's move to start direct talks with Israel suddenly laid bare all these contradictions, however much, at the moment, it looks as though it will be a failure. Should it fail, this would certainly not, however, mean a victory for the opposite tenet. However one looks at the Arab-Palestinian and Arab-Israeli problem, these contradictions remain unaltered, since they are inherent in the fragile structure of the present Arab nations and their socio-political and economic reality.

This is why the Istituto Affari Internazionali considered it worthwhile and appropriate to promote a reassessment of the Arab-Palestinian conflict, as part of its studies on 'stability and development in the Mediterranean'. We asked Walid Kazziha to make a running commentary on a series of events, which resulted in this book, based on comments written between 1974 and 1978 on the course of events. We feel that the result is interesting and serves to open up discussion on the whole Middle Eastern question. It is in this spirit that we present this book, without necessarily sharing his approach or his analysis, but in the certainty of contributing to a better understanding of the political processes operating in the Arab world.

Stefano Silvestri
Istituto Affari Internazionali

INTRODUCTION

The Arab world has for some time now, more specifically since the Balfour Declaration in 1917, known the recurring problem of the Palestinian cause. Often the Palestinian question is seen, especially by some Palestinians who seek self-reliance in their struggle for the achievement of their patriotic aims, as being a separate issue from other problems that engulf the Arab world. One of the debates which ensued after the June 1967 war was precisely concerned with defining the relationship between the Palestinian Resistance Movement and the Arab governments and peoples. Fateh, for example, stressed the idea that there need not be any interference in the affairs of the Palestinians if the Palestinians did not meddle in the political affairs of the Arab countries. Others argued that the Palestinian question was inseparable from other problems which the Arab world faced, namely, imperialism and Zionism; that the political situation in some Arab countries had a direct bearing on the way the Palestinians sought to conduct their national struggle; that the Arab governments have always interfered in the affairs of the Palestinians; and that as long as the Palestinians did not have a territorial base from which to launch their fight, they could not avoid Arab interference.

Historically, a review of the issue under discussion reveals that more often the Palestinian problem has been subject to the political fluctuations of the Arab political scene. Some of the early references made regarding the status of Palestine date back to the First World War. The Arabs in 1915, led by Sharif Hussein claimed Palestine as part of the Hashemite dynasty to be recognised after the Ottoman defeat. Later his son Faysal agreed to endorse the Zionist claim to Palestine. A few years later, another of his sons, Abdullah, promised to take a similar step if the British were willing to assist him in securing the throne of Syria. On a number of occasions the Palestinians were the bargaining card, conveniently bought and sold by the Arab governments to serve the interests of the leadership in some Arab countries. In 1936, when the Palestinians threatened to undermine the position of the Zionist

settlers as well as the British authorities in Palestine, the Arab governments intervened on behalf of their British sponsors to stifle the efforts
of the Palestinian rebels. Similarly, in 1948, seven Arab armies entered
Palestine with the declared intention of saving the Palestinian people
from Zionism, but the war ended with the majority of the Palestinians
turned into a nation of refugees. Moreover, whatever Palestinian land
was not included in the new Zionist state, was annexed by the neighbouring Arab countries. As a result, the West Bank came under the
direct rule of the Jordanian monarch, and the Gaza strip was placed
under the Egyptian military administration. Since then, the leaders
of the Arab states have made a number of attempts to reach an agreement with Israel at the expense of the Palestinian people. In this
context, Abdullah's, and later on his grandson's, regular contacts with
Israel are too well known to deserve any elaboration. Even Nasser made
a determined effort in 1955 to reach a compromise with Israel through
the good offices of the British, but failed. Since 1948, Arab history has
been full of substantiated stories of the betrayal of the Palestinians
by the Arab political leadership.

What is ironic, however, is that today there is a growing wave of
Arab opinion, strongly encouraged by the Arab regimes, asserting
that the Arabs have sacrificed everything for the sake of their Palestinian brothers. Arab governments use every opportunity to remind the
Palestinian people and to impress other Arabs with the false notion
that they have fought so many wars and depleted their economic
resources for the benefit of the Palestinian cause. When such claims
are critically scrutinised it is possible to see that successive Arab governments, since the end of the First World War, have aborted or taken part
in the aborting of the Palestinian efforts for independence and freedom.
The Arab regimes got involved in one war after another and caused the
loss of Palestine piece by piece until they began to lose parts of their
own territories. Last but not least, the Arab regimes have exacted a
higher toll of Palestinian lives than Israel can claim.

A full understanding of the Arab-Israeli conflict requires the unravel-
ling of the contradictions which determine the nature of the hostility
between each Arab country, mainly the front-line Arab countries, and
the state of Israel. It may come as a surprise to many Arabs and foreigners to know that the Palestinians are not always the fundamental cause

of a military clash in the Middle East, nor are they the reason why Arab governments fight their wars against Israel. As a matter of fact the Arab states in 1948 lost a sizeable portion of Palestine, in 1967 they abandoned the rest of it and in 1973, when they fared better on the battlefield, they managed to regain parts of their occupied territories, but had no intention of liberating Palestine.

Nevertheless, whenever the Arab regimes refer to their conflict with Israel, it is always Palestinian interests that they claim to have at heart; but in fact there is more at stake. There are the old and new feuds among the Arab leaders. Some of them, in their effort to gain the wider support of the Arab nation as a whole, tend to champion pan-Arab causes such as Arab unity and the return of the Palestinians to their homeland. Less than a year after the vicious Syrian onslaught on the PLO positions in Lebanon, Hafez Assad hypocritically claimed that there should be 'no bargaining on the rights of the Palestinian people'.* As far as the Arab regimes are concerned, the Palestinian cause is, and has been, a pawn of inter-Arab rivalry. Whenever inter-Arab conflict is intensified, the Palestinian problem gains prominence, but once the Arab leaders make peace with each other even for a short time, the Palestinian cause is brushed under the carpet. This 'competition' among the leaders of the Arab world in the course of promoting their interests internally and on a pan-Arab level has often contributed to miscalculated risks taken by some Arab regimes against Israel.

However, it is fair to say that the basis of the Arab-Israeli conflict is embedded in the inability of both the Arab regimes and Israel to adjust politically and economically to each other. On the one hand, the Arab countries have been subjected to the creation of an alien, in some respects aggressive, political and military entity in their midst, an entity which poses a continuous threat to their sovereignty and long-term existence. On the other hand, since her establishment, Israel has found it difficult to relinquish her aims at expansion and has continued to grasp every opportunity to extend her territorial gains into the neighbouring Arab states.

The following four essays do not purport to produce an in-depth study of the Arab-Israeli conflict. Our concern, however, is to provide the basis for a better understanding of the Palestinian question as one

Guardian, 13 August 1977.

of the political variables which has a direct bearing on the development of events in the region. It is in fact an attempt to answer a basic question: why has the Palestinian question remained with the world for such a long time? And why is it that, when it is least expected, it re-emerges as a central issue in the politics of the region? There have been periods in the recent history of the Arab world when the Palestinian problem has been seen only as that of a displaced community, of a group of refugees in need of resettlement. Following the Arab defeat in 1967, Golda Meir, when asked what she thought should be done with the Palestinians, looked around her and asked: 'Where are they?' Even today some are wondering whether, after the civil war in Lebanon, one can talk about the presence of a Palestinian national movement or not. Yet there have been times when the Palestinians have seemed to be playing a very important political and even military role in the region. Their strength has sometimes provoked some Arab governments to act militarily against them, Jordan in 1970, Lebanon in 1973 and Syria in 1976.

One cannot help wondering if the Palestinians may yet play a crucial role in the future, but the important question is: under what conditions? It is to this question that we address ourselves in these essays. The central theme which runs through them pertains to the fluctuating relationship between the Arab regimes and the Palestinian Resistance Movement. It is within this context that the first essay examines the various factors which have shaped that relationship at different intervals. The second essay focuses on the Lebanese civil war. It is a case study of how the contradictions between the Arab regimes and the Resistance Movement operate in a crisis situation and reach the level of an armed confrontation. The third essay examines the possibilities of peace and war in the region. And the fourth is concerned with Sadat's peace initiative and its consequences on the relations between Egypt and the Palestinian Resistance Movement.

These essays have been written at different times since 1976 and each reflects the political impression of the author at the particular time of writing. This explains why no attempt has been made to modify the content of these essays to suit the new developments. However, the author may modestly claim that his understanding of the issues discussed belongs to the radical academic tradition which has been gaining increasing weight since 1967. To place these essays within a specific academic tradition does not undermine their worth. On the contrary, it charges them with the double burden of interpreting the events and at the same time exposing a way of thinking.

It is the purpose of these essays to present an opposing view of the Arab-Palestinian relations to that of the Arab Establishment (Governments, statesmen, 'nationalised' intellectuals, etc . . .). If that proves to be too ambitious an objective to realise, then some contribution towards the dismantling of the dominant views of the Establishment would be a satisfying achievement.

May 1978

1 THE POLITICAL AND IDEOLOGICAL IMPACT OF THE PALESTINIAN RESISTANCE MOVEMENT ON THE ARAB WORLD SINCE 1967

Introduction

Ideologies in the Arab world have been partly dominated by the process of borrowing intellectual traditions from the West and partly shaped by the major events which have shaken the roots of Arab society in the recent past. More often Arab intellectuals and idealists react either positively or negatively to the flow of Western ideas and concepts and persistently seek to understand the rapid changes which take place in the world around them. The nature of Arab thought has thus become a reactive one, a continuous effort to rationalise what has happened rather than to determine the course of development of events or at least introduce guidelines for the future. Consequently, a gap has been created between the Arabs' attempts to understand and project an image of the future and their efforts to grasp the meaning of present events. Unfortunately, historical events have always rendered any vision of the future obsolete and out-of-date by imposing new situations unaccounted for in their intellectual articulations. Over and over again, the Arabs have been caught unawares because of the shortcomings of their ruling elites and the lack of intellectual initiative among their own intelligentsia. During the last decade two major wars have taken place between the Arabs and Israel and on both occasions most of the Arabs were caught by surprise. It is only after the event that the Arab mind moved to cope with the new situation. New explanations were introduced and new interpretations were elaborated. The whole issue of the Arab-Israeli conflict was reconsidered. One such attempt was made by the Palestinian Resistance Movement (PRM).

It is the contention in this essay that the PRM has since 1967 developed a new pattern of thought in the Arab world which, if allowed to survive, may cause substantial deviation from the old patterns. While Arab political and social thought has in the past been consistently overwhelmed by political events, the PRM with its emphasis on revolutionary thought and action appears to free Arab understanding from some of its static notions and restrictive conceptions of politics and society. The PRM may have not yet produced a blue-print of the future, but the political and intellectual obsessions of the past seem to face a serious challenge to their long-held position. It is further worth noting that in the context of the intellectual climate which emerged after the June war, the PRM has attracted a growing number of Arab intellectuals who are more interested in examining the potentials and prospects of Arab social and political development than accepting the established norms which have the strong and unyielding support of Arab regimes. However, the question remains as to what kind of intellectual climate the last two wars with Israel produced and what the relative weight of the Palestinian ideological stand is compared with other intellectual positions held in the Arab world.

To begin with it is necessary to define the major trends in the Arab understanding of the June war and the October war and the consequent effects of the two wars on the political situation in the Arab world. The scope of the survey is limited by the nature of the literature available on the subject which mainly reflects the views of specific segments of Arab society, namely: the intellectuals, government officials and political leaders. Unfortunately no serious effort has yet been made to gauge the attitude of the Arab masses in different Arab countries. In this respect, the researcher may only rely on speculation and on personal observations and experience. However, this does not exclude the fact that in some cases the formulations and conceptions established before and after the two wars have filtered down to other segments of Arab society.

A case in point is the ongoing process of political indoctrination among the Palestinians in the refugee camps, and the growing impact of the propaganda campaigns conducted by Arab governments which no doubt have reached some segments of the people in the countryside and the urban centres and have come to form part of their political consciousness.

Before addressing ourselves to the main question: the Arab understanding of the recent two Arab-Israeli wars, it is appropriate to note that despite the appearance of an Arab consensus in the summit meeting in Rabat in October 1974, it is safe to say that there is no uniform

Arab official attitude toward Israel or the PRM. As a matter of fact Rabat turned out to be the parting point among the Arabs. Since then the gap has widened between some Arab regimes and others (Syria and Egypt), old enemies have become allies (Syria and Jordan), while old allies have been alienated from each other (PLO and Syria).

The June War

The shocking defeat of the Arabs in the six-day war revealed to them the magnitude of the problems their society had been suffering from for decades, if not centuries. The psychological mobilisation of the Arabs in the days immediately preceding the outbreak of hostilities greatly contributed to the feeling of humiliation and despair which followed. Instead of the long-entertained idea of sweeping victory on the front by the Arab armies described by one of the Arab war ministers at that time as 'the strongest striking force in the Middle East', the outcome of the first few hours of the war left these armies shattered and with them were shattered the hopes of the Arab peoples.

However, the mood of despair did not last long. Partly to reassert their self-respect and partly to find solutions to the catastrophic situation which confronted them, the Arabs gradually adopted four major approaches to account for the underlying cause of the defeat and prescribed remedies to cope with it. The first approach was based on the idea of popular armed resistance. Its main advocates were the Palestinian Organisations. Arab governments, mainly the front-line countries (Syria and Egypt), while admitting some of the merits of the new tendency, were more inclined to opt for an eclectic and conventional solution. According to them there was nothing intrinsically wrong with Arab society. What the situation required was major military adjustments coupled with a new political and diplomatic initiative to strengthen the military front. A third approach was theological and viewed the confrontation between the Arabs and the Israelis as one between the believers and non-believers. Accordingly what was required from the Arabs was strict adherence to the teachings of Islam and a strategy based on the concept of the holy war. The fourth trend which, for lack of a more accurate term, may conveniently be described as a modernist approach, recognised in the defeat a further indication of a continuous process of social and political disintegration in Arab society.

Less than a year after the June war, the Palestinian Resistance Movement led by Fateh was able to make a relatively successful military stand in Karameh, a small refugee camp east of the Jordan river. This was the first sign in the Arab world that alternatives to conventional wars with Israel might be available in a new strategy known as 'the people's liberation war'. Consequently the ranks of Fateh and more than half a dozen other Palestinian organisations were flooded with new recruits from the refugee camps and Arab youth from a number of Arab countries.

The new tendency was reinforced by the adoption in varying degrees of Marxism-Leninism-Maoism as the guiding ideology for political and military action. It provided a theoretically coherent set of ideas which explained the cause of defeat and simultaneously, perhaps more importantly, in the midst of despair it offered hope in the future. Briefly, the analysis went as follows.

The so-called progressive Arab regimes (Egypt, Syria and Iraq) served the interest of the petty bourgeoisie. By its nature this class was hesitant in its political and social behaviour. It failed to confront imperialism and Zionism head-on and refrained from relying on the workers and peasants to introduce a genuine socialist revolution. Its successive wars with Israel proved beyond any doubt that it feared the effective involvement of the toiling and oppressed masses in politics. Thus it did not mobilise them before or even after the war. Moreover, it lacked the determination to fight seriously a war to liberate Palestine. The petty bourgeois regimes more often than not had used the Palestinian issue for purposes of internal consumption and as a means of political blackmail in the context of inter-Arab conflict. The Arab army officers were part and parcel of this class, in fact the iron arm of the petty bourgeoisie. Naturally, they were more interested in enjoying the privileges they had acquired once they were in power rather than fighting the Israelis at the front. Therefore, the only solution to that problem was to organise a mass revolutionary movement which by advocating armed struggle would eventually revolutionalise the whole situation in the Arab world and bring about the downfall of these regimes. To put it more clearly, the way to Tel Aviv had first to pass through the Arab capitals. Fateh while partly accepting this line of thinking was less antagonistic to the Arab regimes. Its members believed that a successful liberation war can only be carried out by the Palestinian masses. In the meantime, the PRM ought to maintain friendly relations with the Arab regimes and avoid entanglement in inter-Arab conflicts.

A less radical reaction to the June war emerged among a number of liberal-minded intellectuals and the apologists of the Arab governments. In the first instance, heads of Arab states, meeting in Khartoum shortly after the war in an attempt to regain some of their self-confidence and salvage their lost credibility and prestige, overreacted to the disastrous event by taking a position of no negotiations with the enemy and no recognition of Israel. A few months later, this was followed by the war of attrition on the Egyptian front. Its purpose was to show that serious steps were being taken to keep the issue alive and present a more respectable image of Arab military capabilities. Under pressure from the angry masses half-hearted measures were taken to punish those who were held to be directly responsible for the defeat. Gradually, an eclectic approach to the understanding of the causes of the set-back emerged.

Accordingly, the whole event was viewed as a result of a series of mistakes, shortcomings, irresponsibility on the part of some individuals and, most important, of the military and technically ill-preparedness of the Arabs. It was, therefore, thought to be most essential in the future that the Arab-Israeli conflict should be taken more seriously by the political leadership of the Arab world and more effort ought to be devoted to the absorption of the advanced techniques of modern warfare. At the same time a calculated move should be made on the political front with the purpose of gaining more friends internationally for the Arab cause and weakening the links between Israel and the USA, its main supporter. This point of view rejected the notion of a people's liberation war on two scores: a) The terrain, especially on the Egyptian front, was not conducive to guerilla warfare. b) The Arabs, instead of severing their links with the West (imperialism) and fighting it head-on, were still in a position to cultivate their relationships with the West including the USA. In this respect, some positive results were to be expected by intensifying the Arabs' diplomatic efforts in the West, co-ordinating and strengthening their propaganda campaign; and, most important, using oil as a political leverage.

The declared 'realistic objective' of the advocates of this moderate approach was 'to wipe out the traces of aggression'. This strategy was based on the following lines:

1. Preservation of Arab solidarity by maintaining close economic, political, and whenever possible, military co-operation between the Arab regimes.
2. Projecting a moderate image of the Arabs in the West and the USA by advocating reasonable demands which did not go beyond the return of the Arab territories lost in 1967, together with a vague formula regarding the legitimate rights of the Palestinian people.
3. Building up the military capabilities of the Arab countries which were to confront Israel in a future war.
4. Accepting the UN resolution 242 which recognises the state of Israel.

The main factor which seemed to undermine these arguments was previous experience and the crisis of confidence between the Arab governments and their peoples. To the Arab layman and intellectual, the issue was more than obvious: 'Our governments have been doping us with such ideas since 1948, but on every occasion, they have failed to deliver the goods. There was no reason to believe that this time, they would do any better.' The result was a feeling of resignation and indifference and the credibility of Arab governments remained as low as ever.

Encouraged by some Arab governments, a third trend evolved advocating an Islamic federation: a form of co-operation between Muslim states to revive the concept of a Muslim community. The ideological and political bases for a move on the part of the Arabs to join hands with non-Arab Muslim countries was twofold. On the one hand, in the face of an increasing tendency adopted by some Arab regimes to introduce a vague form of socialism, other Arab governments felt that this might threaten the vested interests of the ruling groups in their own countries. Their fear was further aggravated by the popularity of Nasser who championed the cause of Arab unity throughout the late 1950s and the 1960s. Against Arab socialism, which was equated to communism, and Nasser's drive for Arab unity the notion of Islamic alliance was posed. Its purpose was to counteract the threat which seemed to undermine the socio-economic and political position of some traditional regimes in the Arab world. Consequently, when Syria and Egypt were defeated in the June war, one of the interpretations which emerged in line with this policy might be summarised in the following words:

> Since the Arabs have deserted religion by adopting communism, God in turn has deserted them. It was inevitable that they should be humiliated at the hands of their enemies, the Jews.

An extreme expression of this view was revealed by one of the sheikhs of the *sufi* orders, who claimed that the defeat was a natural outcome of using arms imported from a communist country.

One would not have been surprised to find a politically illiterate sheikh holding such views, but when a journalist of respectable standing subscribes to a similar theological explanation, one realises to what extent superstitions are still an important factor in shaping the understanding of historical events by some Arabs:

> We have closed our eyes as to the real causes of the defeat. No one mentioned the fact that we had forgotten God and therefore God had forgotten us. That atheism spread among those who claim themselves to be intellectuals . . . Not one single newspaper could reveal that one of the causes of defeat was that there were thousands of political prisoners and internees. That God could not allow us victory with such a large number of innocent people in our prisons.

A fourth approach among a number of intellectuals was one which viewed the whole event in a wider context. The collapse of the Arab armies, political disunity, social fragmentation and corruption were only the symptoms of a more basic malady in Arab society, namely, the inability to confront the modern world with a viable Arab culture. It was not the fault of the army or any particular leader or government, but the whole society and the individual who had lost his self-identity, who as a result of political suppression, deprivation and submission for centuries to superior cultures had been dehumanised, or at least rendered powerless in this world. In fact the problem was not strictly Arab, but engulfed the Third World countries as a whole. The remedy could not be instantaneous, but would require decades, perhaps centuries before the individual and his society underwent a process of total transformation. Obviously this point of view was most pessimistic and held some hope for a solution only in the very remote   future.

These four major trends which appeared after 1967, held in common the idea that there was no quick solution to the Arab dilemma. Time proved even less encouraging than it was first thought to be. The Palestinian Resistance Movement experienced a major crisis, almost a crippling set-back in September 1970 at the hands of the Jordanian army. Its operations against the Israelis were eventually limited to suicidal attacks across the Lebanese borders. Simultaneously, the war of attrition on the Egyptian front came to an end in expectation of an American initiative for a political settlement which never materialised at the time.

Towards the end of 1973, the probability of a military confrontation with Israel seemed more remote than ever, due to the strain in relations with the Soviet Union, Egypt's main arms supplier, and the expulsion of the Russian military mission which was rumoured to have been providing an air cover over Egyptian territory. The prevalent impression was that though Egypt and Syria had been able to build up their armed forces, the Arab regimes were more inclined to search for a political solution than to take a military risk in which the odds were strongly against them. Furthermore, measures to promote Arab solidarity did not seem by 1973 to have reached a level which would allow them to tilt the military balance of power in their favour. Israel backed by the USA continued to pose as the invincible enemy whose military might and political viability internally and internationally was unchallengeable. The Israeli raid on Beirut in 1973 and the incursion of commando units and air strikes deep into Egyptian and Syrian territory confirmed the belief among the Arabs that their armies could in no way match that of Israel.

The October War

In 1973, the state of mind of the Arabs was most pessimistic. Not only did they have no confidence in their armies, but had over and beyond this witnessed for a number of years the deterioration of the 'internal front' resulting from an increasing rate of inflation, widespread corruption, internal political conflicts and the breakdown in some Arab countries of the public services. The obvious conclusion was that if this was the state of affairs along the internal front, then how could the military front be any better? In a public lecture, a prominent Egyptian intellectual told his audience: 'Today we are living in the bottom of a deep well; we cannot go any lower.' One of the audience, a student, asked: 'What do you suggest we do?' The reply was: 'Rebel'.

It would appear that while almost all aspects of Arab life had severely suffered following the June war, one sector, to the surprise of the Arabs and the international community at large seemed to have developed at a rate incomparable with and at the expense of practically all other sectors. The Egyptian and Syrian armed forces had by the beginning of October 1973 completed the preparations that started a year earlier at the orders of the political leadership in both countries to launch a co-ordinated offensive against Israel on two fronts, but with limited political and military objectives.

It is not the purpose of this essay to dwell in any detail on the war operations, but to examine the reactions and attitudes that the October war released among the Arabs. By and large the literature on the subject, with a few exceptions, is superficial. Numerous books and articles are available but seem to scratch only the surface of the subject. However, it is possible to make a few generalisations which depict the main views that have been expressed since October 1973.

The October war caught the Arabs psychologically unprepared for the event. In the first few days of the war the immediate reaction was one of self-restraint mixed with an underlying fear that this was another round with Israel which might ultimately prove to be more damaging than 1967. Those who were a little more optimistic interpreted the event as a game purely designed by the two super-powers and in which their clients in the Middle East played the specific roles assigned to them. They claimed that the essence of the game in the new age of entente was to solve once and for all those problems which carried the seeds of a military confrontation between the super-powers. A well-known Arab economist a day or two before the war, when news of concentration of troops were reported in the Arab press, said 'I would not be surprised if we hear on the radio tomorrow that the Egyptian army has crossed the Canal.' He claimed that a settlement would then ensue in which the Arab governments would be in a position to recognise Israel and at the same time face their own people and say that they had not only wiped out the traces of aggression but also in a daring move got rid of humiliation. Similarly, the Israeli government in return for Arab recognition would be in a position to make substantial territorial concessions without fearing any serious repercussions from its own public opinion. This hypothesis was too neat to be taken seriously and later events on the military front as well as the political level tended to disprove it.

With the first week of the war over, and the Arab forces still holding to their ground, and in some instances even developing their offensive, the mood changed into one of cautious optimism. While in the early days of the war, the Arabs tuned in to foreign broadcasts to follow up the news, by the second week the Egyptian military communiques had gained more credibility. However, when the Israeli forces managed to infiltrate into the West Bank of the Canal during the third week, the element of optimism was neutralised and the cease-fire agreement was received with passive satisfaction and a sense of relief.

These were the short-term transitory responses to the October war. In time more stable reactions appeared, drawing mainly on the ones that have already been discussed in relation to 1967. The first instalments of official and semi-official literature which flooded the Arab world were those which dealt with the military aspects of the war. Most of the emphasis was placed on the meticulous planning for the military operations and the heroic performance of the Arab soldier and officer. There was an attempt to project a new and more prestigious image of the Arab armies in order to replace the old discredited one. Some writers even went so far as to state that the Arab armies did not have the advantage of a surprise attack because the Israelis had already known about it a couple of days earlier and had taken partial precautions. The surprise was a strategic one and not tactical. Since 1967, Israel had fallen into a trap of her own making. Over-confidence in her military strength had deluded her and her allies and prevented her from realising the significance of the Arab military preparations. The idea of Israeli military invincibility was therefore a myth rather than a reality.

On the political level, the Arabs emphasised the point that a strategy based on the idea of territorial security and an expansionist policy in an age when modern warfare became increasingly dependent on electronic equipment and highly sophisticated weapons had been rendered relatively obsolete by the October war. With an eye on the role of the super-powers and the international community in reaching a final settlement, the Arabs were driving home the point that while Israel held on to every inch of land she had occupied in 1967, her bargaining position had become untenable. The guarantee for Israel's security could only be achieved by a peaceful settlement in which she would have to return the lands she had occupied in 1967 and recognise 'the legitimate rights of the Palestinians'.

The war impressed the Arabs with the effectiveness of the use of oil as a political weapon in their efforts to achieve an Israeli withdrawal. It had an immediate impact on the political and even the military position of a number of Western European and Asian countries, towards the Arab-Israeli conflict.

A careful examination of the military and political responses expressed shortly after the war revealed that the eclectic tendency came to dominate the climate of opinion in the Arab world. After all, those who had since 1967 preached the idea that what the Arabs needed was a well-trained army with modern equipment, and advocated that each Arab country contributed what it was willing to give to the war effort, took upon themselves the task of tilting the balance of power in the region in a drastic fashion. It was to the credit of Egypt and Syria that the stalemate in the Middle East was broken. The logical though simple and straightforward proved to be more effective, at least for the time being, than the dialectical, theological or the modernist. However, these remaining tendencies, though weakened, did not disappear altogether; some were modified.

The more radical Marxist-oriented segment of the Palestinian Resistance Movement took the position that, while the October war indicated that the petty bourgeois regimes preserved a measure of military and political potential for survival, in the final analysis they had betrayed the cause of the Palestinian people and accepted an American solution. Libya and Iraq for political and ideological reasons opted for a similar radical stand and advocated the continuation of the fight until all the Palestinian land was liberated. Gadhafi, shortly after Sadat's acceptance of the cease-fire sent the latter the following bitter cable:

Sir President, if we had fought this war to regain the territories we had lost in 1967, we ended up by accepting the cease-fire without liberating it. If, on the other hand, we had fought to restore our dignity, we had accepted its further humiliation at the 101 km . . . [Reference here is to the direct military negotiations between Israel and Egypt for the withdrawal of the Israeli troops from the West bank of the Suez Canal.]

. . . It would have been more honourable for us if we had continued the fight even with swords, in the mountains, in the woods and in the open, without oil, electricity, towns or politics, but with dignity, honour, religion and Arabism. The land may fall and buildings may collapse, but honour remains.

Eventually, Iraq, Libya and the Popular Front for the Liberation of Palestine came to form part of what is known today as 'the Front of Rejection'. The choice that the Front poses is limited, either all of Palestine with no concessions to American imperialism and Zionism or a protracted war of liberation.

On the other hand, the bulk of the Palestinian Resistance Movement led by Fateh and encouraged by the rest of the Arab countries took a moderate stand. In the conference of the PLO held in Cairo in 1974 it was decided to accept the establishment of a 'Palestinian Patriotic Sovereignty' over any part of Palestine won by negotiations. In October of that year, the Arab summit meeting in Rabat reiterated its recognition of the PLO as the only legitimate representative of the Palestinian people and urged Yasir Arafat to go ahead and institutionalise the Palestinian Movement by forming a government in exile. To some extent, the Palestinian revolution had been tamed or as the Front of Rejection had claimed it had been 'nationalised by the Arab governments'. The recent events in Lebanon have undoubtedly left Fateh with one clear choice: to join hands with the radicals and fight for survival and independence against the attempts at containing it or co-opting it by Arab governments, acting independently (Syria) or jointly (Arab League forces).

Those who had found in Islam a refuge which explained to them the defeat and pointed to the path of salvation applauded the move to liberate the occupied territories in October. For some of them the mere fact that when the Egyptian soldiers after crossing the Canal had praised God's name 'Allah Akbar' was enough indication that a return to faith had been made.

Without it there could have been no victory. Others saw in October a landmark, the beginning of an attempt to liberate the Muslim world from the banner of two centuries of a new Christian crusade, the purposes of which was to destroy Islamic values. According to one of the advocates of such a line of thought the October war had not only changed the military balance in the area, but had actually tipped the scale in favour of Islam. In an alarmist fashion, he claimed that the USA, in an effort to protect its oil interests in the area, might effect a military coup in Saudi Arabia, the cradle and protector of Islam. The wider objectives of the coup in the context of the Islamic-Christian conflict would be twofold: a) to conquer the heart of Islam by imposing Western cultural values and introducing the worst aspects of Western civilisation including night clubs and missionary schools; b) to liquidate the role of the Saudi dynasty as the leading spirit of the Islamic world in Asia and Africa.

However, on balance it would seem that since 1967, and more specifically since Nasser's death in 1970, Saudi Arabia had gradually moved to co-operate closely with Egypt and Syria. The eclectics and conservatives in the Arab world, now that the wave of 'socialism' had receded, or at least the attempt to export socialism from one Arab country to another had become less likely, found that the causes of their disagreement in the past had been eliminated. The October war simply cemented this relationship and reinforced the grounds of co-operation. The eclectics who were in the front line set the pace politically and militarily while the conservatives were satisfied with their economic role which allowed them a great measure of political influence in the Arab world.

The position of the modernists did not undergo any substantial change after October. Following a short period of exultation they reverted to their earlier pessimistic temperament. They soon realised that what they had at first mistaken as the 'return of the soul' was nothing but a partial, military victory. The problems of the past had come to stay for some time. The crisis in Arab society was one which had no cure at the hands of governments or any one individual. It was a case of a patient who had no one to help him except himself, a most difficult task to perform, but one which in time might be possible.

Conclusion

The October war may have widened the basis of internal political support of the Arab regimes which were directly involved in the fighting. In an area where there is no concensus of opinion on a set of rules for the legitimisation, transformation and acquisition of political power, the achievements of Egypt and Syria during the war had stabilised the political situation in both countries and consolidated the position of the political leadership. The war further introduced into the Arab world a new sense of pan-Arabism. This is based on the idea of economic, political and military co-ordination and co-operation between the different kinds of Arab governments, instead of the old concept of Arab unity based on the social and political integration of the Arab peoples. This new sense of pan-Arabism may have little popular support, but the idea certainly appeals to most Arab regimes which are interested in maintaining the political *status quo*.

The Arab masses on the other hand, after a short-lived period of optimism which prevailed during the early days of the October war, reverted to their main concerns of coping with the daily problems facing them, chiefly poverty. The widely advertised open door economic policy and the unprecedented huge revenue accruing from oil had at one time raised their expectations. But in view of the fact that neither Arab capital from the oil-producing countries nor American aid had arrived in the proportions or at the pace expected, the front-line countries continued to suffer from what amounted to a severe economic crisis. In a recent book published in Cairo, entitled *What after the October War?* one of the contributors — an economist — warned:

> The enthusiasm of the masses for an open door economic policy is greater than the realities of the situation . . . At the same time the official announcements made regarding that policy have been out of proportion to anything achieved in that direction. Naturally this is a mistake. Our duty is not to drown the masses in hope . . . because hope may turn into an obsession and an obsession into a mirage.

Despite the relative military and political success of the Arab regimes in October 1973, the revolutionary ideological stand of the PRM seems to have had a more lasting effect on Arab intellectuals than the eclectic and convential one sponsored by the Arab governments. Events in the region since October 1973 have increasingly shown that the axis of inter-Arab conflict has gradually been shifting to a position where the major political and military confrontation is between the PRM and some of the Arab regimes. It is tolerably clear that before the June war the Palestine question had always been used by the Arab ruling elites and governments to embarrass each other in the course of their struggle for power. Each Arab country at one time or another pretended to act as the sole protector of the Palestinian people and the champion of the Palestinian cause. However, after the defeat of 1967 and the emergence of the PRM as a recognised political and military force in the area, the relationship between the Arab regimes and the Palestinians drastically changed. Arab governments were unable from then on to play the patronising role they had played for almost two decades.

By 1968, the PLO had come to represent the hopes and aspirations of the Palestinian people. The Arab regimes did not refrain from making every effort to exploit the differences between the Palestinian groups and organisations for their own purposes, but the process had become much more complicated and difficult than before, especially since Fateh and other Palestinian organisations continued to assert their organisational and ideological independence. As a matter of fact, in some instances the PLO appeared to reverse the nature of the relationship by utilising Arab governments for its own ends. For example, in September 1970 Syria was drawn into a military confrontation with Jordan following King Hussein's successful move to dislodge the Palestinian commandos from Amman and other major towns in Jordan. Early in 1976, the Palestinians gained Syria's support in their effort to discredit the Egyptian regime for concluding the second Sinai agreement. Similarly, when the conflict between the PLO and Syria erupted a few months later as a result of the latter's assistance to the right-wing forces in Lebanon, the PLO patched up its differences with Egypt in an attempt to undermine the position of the Syrian regime.

However, it would appear that despite the transitory nature of the alliances and conflicts between the Arab regimes and the PRM, a basic

and unresolved contradiction does exist between them. This contradiction remains operative on the political, military and ideological levels.
In essence the PRM poses as a serious threat to the existence and per-
petuation of the Arab regimes. For one thing, it has the potential of
becoming a model for political action in the Arab world. While for
years political changes in the area have taken place through conspira-
tional military groups, the adoption of the principle of armed struggle
and popular armed resistance introduces new means of change which
tend to undermine the position of most Arab ruling elites and classes.
It does not only invite the active and open participation of the Arab
masses, but also establishes under certain conditions a new basis of
political legitimacy, one which is based on massive violence and revolutionary activity. All Arab governments, without any exception, would
find such a conception of legitimacy a most embarrassing proposition
to accept or even entertain, no matter how much lip-service some Arab
governments pay to the concept of revolution.

Perhaps a more immediate danger to the position of the Arab regimes
is the PRM's deliberate disregard for the political and territorial sovereignty of some Arab countries. The PRM has persistently subordinated
the territorial integrity of some Arab countries, namely, Syria, Lebanon
and Jordan to the specific demands of the Palestinian Revolution. This
lay at the roots of the conflict between the Jordanian regime and the
PLO in 1970; and it also remains the major outstanding issue in Lebanon
between the contending parties.

Since the First World War and the creation of several political entities with recognised boundaries and systems of government in the Arab
East, a number of political movements have emerged in the area with
the aim of uniting its separate parts under the sovereignty of one state
structure. However, the ruling elites in each of the Arab countries were
continually able to assert their independent position and successfully
resisted all attempts at unification. They managed to withstand the
pressures exerted upon them by the pan-Arab and pan-Syrian movements. Even the limited success of Nasserism in Syria in 1958 was
short-lived before Syrian particularism reasserted itself and broke the
first concrete attempt at Arab unification. In time, identification with
a specific territory and a growing sentiment toward regionalism came
to form part of the political reality in the area. State boundaries and

national sovereignty became sacred elements in the life of the separate Arab entities. Undoubtedly many Arab governments continued to praise the cause of Arab integration and political unification, but the fact of the situation was that most of the Arab governing elites realised that they had a lot to lose if they allowed regional boundaries to disappear and new political elites sponsoring the cause of unity to emerge. While the PRM did not emphasise the idea of Arab unity nevertheless, due to its military attacks against Israel, it tended to jeopardise the sovereignty of the Arab countries around Palestine by inviting Israeli retaliatory action. After an initial period of tolerance, the patience of these Arab regimes was further exacerbated by yet another, in some cases more serious, threat to their sovereignty. This was the presence on their territory of armed groups of Palestinians who did not abide by the state laws and almost created a situation of a state within a state. Sooner or later a confrontation was inevitable between the recognised state authorities and the newly established armed forces of the Resistance Movement. In short, none of the Arab countries was willing in the long run to sacrifice, even in part, its recently earned statehood for the sake of what is often claimed to be the Arabs' most sacred cause: Palestine.

Moreover, the Arab countries have for some time been searching for an internal arrangement, a social and political formula which would allow them a measure of internal stability and a viable political structure. So many experiments have been tried under the mandatory power and since the independence of a number of Arab countries after the Second World War. These experiments ranged from the installation of democratic systems of government with certain limitations to absolute forms of monarchies and dictatorships. In practically every case, even when a change of government occurred through a military coup, the governing groups or individuals immediately moved to introduce a constitution or a set of laws and regulations to safeguard the newly won position they had acquired. Invariably, this implied a strict notion of law and order which rarely tolerated opposition or antagonism to the established authorities. Even the so-called revolutionary parties, such as the Baath in Iraq and Syria, once in power exerted every effort to codify the measures they had introduced and thus left very little room for legitimate political change to take place in the future. The result has often been the suppression of any political opposition to the point of physical liquidation and the elimination of any political activity which might undermine the stability of the existing regime. The PRM is an anathema to such a notion of political stability. By its very nature, organisationally and ideologically, it is the complete opposite of what the Arab regimes stand for in terms of political stability and ideological uniformity. The PRM does not only consist of a number of competing organisations, but also represents a variety of ideological tendencies. Within the context of the political situation in the Arab world it is a most tolerant movement and, therefore, less amenable to Arab pressures which seek to tailor its development and progress in accordance with the different interests of the Arab regimes. As a revolutionary movement still in the process of struggle for existence it does not lend itself to a rigid form of codification. Law and order, stability and uniformity are somewhat alien to it. More to the point, it embodies the negation of such notions.

Undoubtedly the Arab regimes are not willing to coexist with such a disruptive political and military force in their midst. 'A Revolution until Victory,' a major aim of the Palestinian Revolution raised by Fateh and shared by the rest of the movement, may only be achieved through the dismantling of the political and social fabric adopted by a number of Arab countries. In the final analysis, the conflict between the Arab regimes and the PRM is one between defined concepts of political legitimacy and a more elusive and revolutionary form of political organisation and action, an attachment to the idea of national sovereignty and a tendency to ignore internationally recognised boundaries; and ultimately it is a conflict between the Arab regimes which are keenly interested in preserving the *status quo* and a revolutionary movement which seeks to transform it.

August 1976

2 THE LEBANESE CIVIL WAR AND THE PALESTINIAN RESISTANCE MOVEMENT

The eruption of the civil war in Lebanon in 1975, has been described by observers of the Arab scene as a conflict between the Muslim left and the Christian right, a sectarian and socio-economic conflict. Some viewed the confrontation as one between pan-Arabism and Lebanese nationalism; in other words an ideological confrontation. Still, others laid emphasis on the politico-ethnic aspect of the conflict and saw it as one between the Lebanese and 'foreigners' represented by the Palestinians. Some even entertained the idea of a clash between Soviet and American interests in the area.

There is some truth in most of these interpretations; however, unless some effort is made to analyse the different components of the Lebanese crisis, a very confusing and misleading image of the situation might arise. This is a tentative attempt to study the recent violent upsurge in Lebanon in the light of the accumulative effects of a number of changes which had taken place in Lebanese society and led to rendering the so-called 'Lebanese formula' redundant and obsolete.

The Lebanese Formula

Since 1943, the ruling class in Lebanon including a reasonable segment of intellectuals and scholars had prided themselves on the fact that Lebanon had moved a long way towards modernisation without resort to radical changes. The 'Lebanese Formula', better known as the 'National Pact', had often been referred to as the corner-stone of Lebanon's political stability and the driving force of Lebanese progress.

> The slow gains accomplished, step by step, in cultural, economic, and political spheres are the results of stable political institutions and of a formula for government based on conciliation and consensus.[1]

In effect the National Pact was a communal compromise between the Christians, more specifically the Maronite community leaders,

39

basically isolationists with strong pro-Western sympathies, and the Muslims, especially the Sunni pan-Arab leadership, to recognise a fully independent Lebanon with Arab attachments. The first president of the Republic after independence and one of the architects of the Pact expressed the essence of the compromise by saying:

> Lebanon wants its complete independence within its present boundaries; and we want, on this basis, to co-operate with the Arab States to the greatest possible extent.[2]

What these words failed to reveal was the fact that, apart from being a formula for co-operation and coexistence between the two major religious communities in Lebanon, the National Pact was also an expression of the social and economic forces dominant in Lebanese society at the time.

It is generally accepted that the Lebanese economy is an economy of services, whereby this particular sector forms over 68 per cent of the GDP. Traditionally, the merchants of Beirut and the coastal towns, predominantly Sunnis, had been closely associated with the Arab hinterland. Sunni merchants and town notables had been instrumental, since independence, in expanding Lebanon's trade and business links with the rest of the Arab countries especially Syria, Iraq, and Jordan and since the oil bonanza with Saudi Arabia and the Gulf states. Many of them through intermarriage had developed social and economic ties with the leading families of Damascus and Aleppo. More recently, a large number of Muslim young men had moved east to find employment in Saudi Arabia and the Gulf, while over 60 per cent of Lebanon's exports found their way to Arab markets. The Maronite businessmen and merchants, on the other hand, had close relationships with the West. They imported goods from the West and through their Sunni contacts sold them to other Arabs. Many of them were able financiers who made use of the inflow of oil money and managed to develop Beirut as the financial centre of the Middle East.

The National Pact put paid to the marriage between the two business communities in Lebanon.

Prelude to 1975

From 1943 to 1975, Lebanon witnessed the growth of new social and political forces which eventually threatened the whole fabric of society and the system of government established in the 1940s. One major development had been the numerical increase in the size of the Shi'i community to a point where it became the largest single sect.[3] In itself this would have posed no serious problems. It was only when a growing number of educated Shi'is became dissatisfied with the system and large numbers of poorer Shi'is moved to the towns, particularly Beirut, that a sharp social and political problem gradually emerged. Neither the Pact with its limitations on the proportion of Shi'is employed in government administration nor the expansion of the services economy was able to absorb this growing number of less well-to-do Shi'is. Professor Salem admitted that the Shi'is in South Lebanon were the people to benefit least from economic prosperity.[4] Many of them moved at different intervals during the 50s and 60s to the suburbs of Beirut in search of employment on the fringes of the services sector and were hardly able to make ends meet.

In a survey carried out by a team from the Lebanese daily *al-Nahar* to investigate the social conditions of the Shi'i quarters around Beirut, which had been involved in the heaviest rounds of fighting and which were often referred to in the international press as the 'belt of misery', the following observations were made:

1. In al-Shiyyah quarter, the majority of the inhabitants suffered from a high rate of unemployment and undernourishment. The average number of people living in one room was ten. On the other hand, Ain al-Rummana quarter, inhabited by a majority of Maronites and separated from al-Shiyyah by an eight-metre-wide road had an average of seven persons living in one house. Most of its inhabitants had employment in some 2000 commercial firms and 600 small industries.[5]

2. Al-Nab'a quarter, another Shi'i slum area had a population of 100,000 inhabitants before it was overrun by the Phalange forces last summer. The majority of them, some 80 per cent, were landless

peasants who emigrated from South Lebanon. '13 per cent of the families of al-Nab'a live in one room, and 20 per cent of these rooms accommodate approximately 10 persons.' According to the only medical doctor in the area the inhabitants suffered continuously from illness caused by hunger and cold. 'A large percentage of the children are unable to walk before the age of five' while 90 per cent of the women were anaemic and lacked calcium.[6]

3. Al-Maslakh and Karintina were undoubtedly the most deprived areas around Beirut. Immediately after they were occupied by the Phalange forces in late 1975, they were levelled to the ground and the Maronite monastic order claimed the ownership of the land. Eighty-five per cent of the inhabitants lived in tin huts which on average accommodated eight to fourteen persons each. The two quarters had no running water or electricity and practically no educational facilities.[7]

The Shi'i emigration to Beirut and the depressing social and economic conditions under which they lived presented the radical movements with the ideal grounds for recruiting an increasing number of political supporters. As a result, a deprived religious group in the economic and social sense was transformed into a politically active and militant community. A leading sheikh described the emergence of an armed militia among the Shi'is in the following words:

The movement emerged as a result of the suffering of the people who were living under the worst conditions of corruption and a minimum standard of a decent life.
On top of this, our people in South Lebanon were continuously threatened in their existence by Israeli aggression. On the other hand, our government's policy was one of neither defending the South nor developing it economically. Consequently a belt of poverty was created around Beirut. It included a group of people who were emigrants from the Beq'a and the South searching for means of livelihood.

When asked where his followers were trained, the following discussion ensued:

> 'Wherever there is deprivation.'
> 'In Beirut?'
> 'Wherever the deprived exist we have training camps.'
> 'Where do you get arms from?'
> 'Our sons deprive even their own children of food to buy arms.'
> 'And trainers?'
> 'We co-ordinate with the Palestinian Resistance and this is no secret. In addition we have some retired army personnel who sympathise with us.'[8]

A qualified observer of the Lebanese scene summed up the conditions around Beirut in the following words:

> Six hundred thousand people are crowded into the 'belt of misery' which strangles Beirut and her suburbs. In the financial metropolis of the Middle East, where banks crumble under the weight of uninvested cash liquidity, more than one-third of the population subsists on the brink of famine. The mortality rate there is two to three times the national average. Low-paid workers and the unemployed alike find it difficult to feed themselves due to exploding prices. Decent housing is nearly out of reach as rents have tripled in two years due to real estate speculation. For their children, schooling and medical care are virtually out of reach.[9]

The Palestinians

The Palestinian presence in Lebanon is estimated at 350,000, of whom some 90,000 live in refugee camps. Before 1967, the Palestinians did not carry any significant political weight in Lebanon. As a matter of fact a sergeant in the Deuxième Bureau (Army Intelligence) was often able, according to the widely used phrase among the inhabitants of the camps 'to close the whole camp' by his sheer arrival at the site. Palestinians were aware of the old days when lieutenant Joseph Kilani, incidentally a Maronite, of the Deuxième Bureau would without inhibitions humiliate 'the biggest head' in any of the refugee camps and arrest any of its inhabitants. After 1967, the situation radically changed.

In the first instance, after the June war, the Arabs viewed with great admiration the emergence of the Resistance Movement and held it as a symbol of Arab defiance against Israel and the USA. The Arab regimes, defeated and discredited, competed among each other to win its blessings. In such an atmosphere of euphoria it was hardly conceivable that any of the Arab governments would try and emasculate the new movement. Soon enough with the influx of armed Palestinians into Lebanon, especially after September 1970, a dual power situation evolved. Whereas the Jordanian regime was successful in reasserting its territorial sovereignty, the Lebanese government failed to do so. In 1969, the Lebanese regime made an attempt to contain the Resistance Movement by force, but when this failed a compromise was reached. Under the auspices of Nasser, an agreement was concluded in Cairo by which the Palestinians extracted 'formal recognition of their autonomous presence in the country and of their right to engage in operations from Lebanese territory subject to the principle of "co-ordination" with the government'[10] In April 1973, under the pretext of putting an end to Palestinian excesses, the Lebanese army received instructions from President Franjieh to launch a co-ordinated attack against the Resistance's strongholds in the midst of the Muslim quarters in Beirut. The army's operation ended in a miserable failure, and the Palestinians in Lebanon once more consolidated their position through reaffirming the Cairo Agreement.

One major consequence of the event was the realisation on the part of the Maronites that without developing their own military strength, there was little prospect for them to regain their political supremacy. Another was a growing awareness among the Palestinians and their Muslim supporters that the army belonged to one group of Lebanese, namely the Christians, rather than to the nation as a whole. No such vigilance was ever exercised by the Lebanese army when the Shi'is in the South and Lebanese sovereignty were threatened by Israel. Both parties, the Maronites on the one hand and the Palestinian-Muslim coalition on the other seemed to work in a direction which had the ultimate result of undermining the authority of the central government. In the meantime, the more radical forces in Lebanon appeared to take advantage of the situation by aligning themselves with the Resistance

Movement and opting for a programme of political and social reform based on an entirely new formula.

The Left

Until very recently, the left in Lebanon has had very little impact on the development of political and social events in the country. The Communist Party founded in the 30s remained for decades a marginal political force unable to command any significant following except among a minority of workers and a small number of intellectuals and students. Its appeal to the Lebanese masses had been negligible due to the adoption of a strategy which often emphasised Soviet interests in the region to the exclusion of the national concerns of the peoples of the area. Undoubtedly the fact that the political and economic organisation of Lebanon was based on confessional grounds tended to militate against a purely secular movement. During the 1950s and 1960s, a new force emerged in the area operating under the banner of Nasserism and Baathism. The new movement while giving the cause of Arab unity paramount importance preached the idea of social justice and economic equality. However, with the failure of the first experiment in Arab unity, following Syria's recession from the UAR in 1961, radical Arab nationalists and communists began to focus their attention on the internal social and economic conditions in each Arab country. Consequently splits began to take place and new inward-looking political groups emerged seeking the achievement of social and economic transformation in their own societies. By 1965, the movement of Arab nationalism in Lebanon had given birth to a number of left-wing organisations which together with the Communist Party and Junblat's Progressive Socialist Party formed a political front advocating mild political and social reforms. A keen interest in the welfare of the workers and small peasants was developed and from the mid-sixties onward the left in Lebanon did not lose any opportunity to champion the cause of the lower classes. Mass rallies were regularly held in support of the small farmers to market their produce at more reasonable prices than the ones offered by the merchants who had a monopoly over agricultural exports. Very often security forces were called upon to intervene in breaking the strikes in factories around Beirut. Young radicals fought side by side with the workers in the tobacco industry as the latter barricaded themselves in the premises of the company. Students were similarly mobilised in the Lebanese, American and Arab universities in Beirut in support of trade union demands. The most serious incident took place in late February 1975, when the left led the fishermen in Beirut, Saida and Tripoli in a series of demonstrations against a newly established company with wide fishing rights owned by ex-President Shamoun. Clashes between the army and protesters at the end of a two-week general strike in Saida culminated in the death of some 24 persons, including leftist leader and former parliamentary deputy Maruf Saad. The left blamed the authorities for the incident.[12]

The involvement of the left-wing organisations in trade union disputes and demands won them the following they had been yearning for for years. Membership in these organisations rapidly increased and new cadres were formed in different parts of the country most notably in the coastal towns, the south, the Baqa'a valley, the Shi'i quarters around Beirut and the mountain villages south of the Beirut-Damascus highway. Some of the organisations, particularly the Communist Party and the Organisation of Communist Action managed to penetrate into a number of Greek Orthodox villages. In the meantime, the remnants of the Nasserite movement regrouped themselves into three active organisations, most important among them the Marabitun, headed by Ibrahim Qulailat. It commanded the loyalty of a sizeable segment of the Sunni middle classes in Saida and Beirut. The Nasserites made a common cause with the left on the basis of their antagonism to the Lebanese formula and their support for the Palestinian Resistance.

From 1965 to 1970, a new bloc in Lebanese politics had emerged, the Progressive Bloc. It represented a coalition between the left with its growing popular base among the lower Muslim classes and the Nasserites and Baathists representing the Sunni middle classes. The role of Kamal Junblat in this coalition was unique compared to other Lebanese Zaims. While maintaining his traditional power base among the Druzes, he was able to extend his political appeal to the poorer Muslim classes by sponsoring the demands of the deprived and championing the cause of the Palestinians in Lebanon. Junblat became the spokesman of the left, its patron and leader. Once the Progressive Bloc appeared on the political scene it gradually acquired teeth through its close association with the Palestinian Resistance Movement.

The Progressive Bloc plus the Resistance Movement

Lebanon entered the seventies with an explosive situation which eventually disrupted the whole fabric of society. The Lebanese Formula and the mystical optimism which had been woven around it proved to be so fragile to the extent that the very political and economic existence of the country appeared to be rapidly disintegrating. Even as late as 1973, the ruling class in Lebanon as well as some scholars and intellectuals continued to underestimate the impact of the new forces of change. Professor Salem wrote:

> Radicals often disagree on policy matters and lack sufficient organisation on party lines to pose a serious danger to the prevailing political order.[13]

It was during that same year that the radical movement in Lebanon cemented its links with the Palestinian Resistance as the latter fought successfully to repel the first serious onslaught of the Lebanese regime against it. After each encounter with the Lebanese government and the Christian militia, the new forces of change, namely the Progressive Bloc and the Resistance Movement, found additional grounds for maintaining a common front against their opponents. Closer links were formed on every level. The Shi'is, who in the first instance blamed the Palestinians for Israeli reprisals in the South, soon realised that abandoned by the central government in Beirut they had no one to turn to except the armed Palestinians who lived among them in the villages and the nearby refugee camps. After a period of hostility, friendly relationships were forged between the two communities, and the Shi'i lower classes turned to the Palestinian organisations for arms and military training. Soon enough, the radical segment of the Palestinian Resistance actively adopted the political and economic demands of the Shi'i community. In return the Shi'i masses moved hand in hand with the left to provide a Lebanese front for the protection of the Palestinian military and political presence in Lebanon. Such a relationship was further consolidated by the organisational arrangements made between the Palestinian Resistance and the Lebanese patriotic and progressive parties. The pro-Iraqi faction of the Baath Party co-ordinated its activities with the Arab

Liberation Front, while the pro-Syrian faction of the Baath co-operated with the Syrian-sponsored al-Sa'iqa Organisation. Similarly the organisation of Communist Action devoted much of its energies in support of the Palestinian Democratic Front and jointly published the weekly *al-Hurriyya*, while the PFLP headed by George Habash was most instrumental in founding the Arab Labour Party. The Communist Party, the Progressive Socialist Party and the Nasserite organisations formed a front in support of Fateh.

Thus no matter how hard an attempt was made, especially by Fateh, to separate the internal crisis of Lebanese society from the Palestinian question the two had become the inextricable components of the same problem. The mechanism of the situation was quite simple. Once the Lebanese order posed against the Resistance, the Lebanese progressive forces were immediately alerted and rallied to the support of the Palestinians. On the other hand, whenever the Lebanese regime attempted to suppress the radical movement, the Palestinian Resistance came to its aid and viewed such a move as a preliminary step towards the isolation and final liquidation of the armed presence of the Palestinians in Lebanon.

The Maronite Front

The Lebanese ruling class and the Maronite community were ultimately faced with one of two choices; either to sit back and watch their position being gradually eroded or confront their opponents both Lebanese and Palestinians at one and the same time. It would appear that a combination of external and internal political and military factors made the latter option sometime around the beginning of 1975 more plausible. The first serious armed clash which triggered off a series of violent rounds took place on 13 April 1975, when a group of Palestinians returning to Tel al-Zaatar refugee camp from a political rally were ambushed by the Phalange militia in Ain al-Rummana.

The Maronite community had since independence gained a predominant position in the political and economic life of the country. At the head of the Lebanese political hierarchy stood a Maronite president with a network of well-established members of his own community placed in positions of power. First among them was the commander of the army and the top-ranking officers. According to a study published by *al-Amal*, the organ of the Phalange Party, Maronite officers formed 36 per cent instead of the 28 per cent allotted to their community in the Lebanese officers corps.[14] Furthermore, the system of political favouritism allowed the president to appoint his close followers to the higher echelons of the civil administration and even create new posts for them when such posts were not available. President Franjieh, throughout his term of office, did not refrain from exploiting this advantage to the point of alienating even some members of his own family including his brother Abdel Hamid Franjieh. Economically, the Christian community and more specifically the Maronites as a whole, being the largest single Christian sect, benefited most from an economy dominated by the financial and services sector. According to Professor Sayigh out of a 'sample of 207 entrepreneurial businessmen, only one sixth were Muslims, . . .'. In addition 'The early Christian dominance of the trade and finance sectors of the economy helped to maintain the upward mobility of the Christian petty bourgeoisie . . . In Beirut, the Christian petty bourgeoisie was demonstrably larger and better off than its Muslim counterpart . . .'[15]

In the agricultural sector political and economic developments since the mid-nineteenth century in Mount Lebanon 'stimulated a growth of peasant proprietorship' among the Christian farmers, thus weakening the hold of the feudal landlords. On the other hand, such a process of social and economic transformation 'was impossible in the predomin-antly Shi'ite Muslim region cut off geographically and culturally from the educational and commercial revolution in Beirut'.[16] In industry the Christians tended to be the proprietors of the larger factories which employed cheap Muslim, Syrian and Palestinian labour. In the industrial region around the famous Tel al-Zaatar camp in north-east Beirut, the scene of the bloodiest battles that took place in the civil war, were located 29 per cent of the factories of Lebanon with a capital forming 23 per cent of the total industrial capital. In this same region were employed 22 per cent of Lebanon's workers most of whom were drawn from the nearby Shi'i quarter al-Nab'a and the Palestinian camps of Jisr al-Pasha and Tel al-Zaatar.[17] The owners of the factories included such well-known Christian bourgeois families as Thabet, Tutanji, Huweik, Fulayfel, 'Aql, Faddul and 'Usayli together with a few well-to-do Sunni families.

The Christian social pyramid emerged with a base confined to a wide petty bourgeois class and independent cultivators. The poorer classes of Lebanon including the workers, and the small and landless peasants formed the base of the Muslim social pyramid. But this was not all; the Christian social structure was historically reinforced by the evolution of an ideology which rested on the concept of a compact community encouraged by the Maronite church under the hegemony of leading families and which had more recently acquired a 'populist' appeal among the independent Christian farmers. According to Albert Hourani, 'In a sense, the Phalanges of today can be seen as heirs of this (latter) tradition.'[18] This ideology did not only provide the Maronites with a self-image, but also determined their perception of the others, namely the Muslims:

> The Maronite common man felt very different from the Moslem. He never did like him. He seemed to tolerate him; but in fact he did not tolerate him as much as he ignored him, And he could ignore him as long as this Moslem did not threaten to challenge his factual, or imaginary position of power.[19]

The Muslims, on the other hand, had traditionally been attached to a pan-Arab ideology. Their commitments had often been made to Arab movements and governments outside Lebanon's borders. Thus an ideological mosaic had emerged among the Muslims extending from moderate forms of pan-Arabism to extreme brands of Marxism-Leninism.

As the Palestinian Resistance began to entrench itself in Lebanon, the Maronites pinned their hopes on the intervention of the army to put a limit to it. In 1973, such hopes in the Lebanese army disappeared into thin air. On the one hand, the army did not prove to be a match for the Palestinians and on the other, signs of dissension appeared among its rank and file and finally led to its disintegration. At that point, the Phalange Party acting as the spearhead of the Maronite community and representing the bulk of the Maronite petty bourgeoisie moved to face the challenge which in effect threatened the supremacy of their community. Bashir Jumayyil, the military leader of the Phalange, dated the confrontation between the party militia and the

Palestinians to 1970 in Kahhale east of Beirut. Since then the party had begun to establish training camps for the purpose of 'self-defence' but by April 1975, Jumayyil claimed that his men were using heavy arms.[20]

The Confrontation

In 1975, the two competing blocs posed against each other for a final show-down: the radicals versus the conservative forces who opted for the *status quo*; the Muslim poor against the petty bourgeois and rich Christians; the advocates of pan-Arabism against Lebanese particularism; and the Palestinians and their left-wing allies in opposition to the Maronite Front. The former advocated two main demands: the complete freedom of the Resistance Movement to operate from Lebanese territory and the introduction of social and political reforms which would redress the balance between the different sectarian groups. The latter, feeling threatened by these two demands both on the socio-economic and political levels, claimed that international communism was conspiring against Lebanon's independence. The leader of the Phalange Party and the Maronite leaders including the President of the Republic accused Junblat and the Palestinian Resistance of being the agents of international communism and Zionism.

The fighting in Lebanon passed into three main phases. The first phase from April 1975 until the end of the year was characterised by a war of positions. The dominant feature of the conflict was the continual sporadic shelling of Muslim border-line areas by the Christian forces and vice versa. During that time, fighting broke out in Beirut along the Shiyyah-Ain al-Rummana axis and in the luxury seaside hotel district. Another front was opened in the north between Tripoli and Zghorta, Franjieh's home-town. On the part of Fateh there was some serious hesitation from entering a full-fledged battle against the Maronite Front. This, however, did not prevent the smaller radical Palestinian organisations from joining hands with the forces of the Progressive Bloc.

The second phase of the fighting began early in January when a co-ordinated offensive was launched by the Maronite forces and showed clear signs of moving towards the partitioning of the country. The Christian side systematically moved to wipe out the Palestinian and Shi'i enclaves in their midst. First to go was the small refugee camp of Dubay near Jounich. It was followed by the massacre of large numbers of Shi'is and Palestinians in the Maslakh and Karantina quarters. Simultaneously, a blockade was imposed on the Tel al-Zaatar and Jusral-Pasha refugee camps. This ushered in a new stage in the development of the fighting, in which Fateh was drawn into the battle in full force so as to protect some 16,000 Palestinians and 54,000 Shi'is in and around the Tel al-Zaatar area. On 18 January, the Lebanese Sunni Prime Minister resigned in objection to the deployment of the air force against the Palestinian forces attacking the Christian town of Damour south of Beirut. On the same day, the Phalange forces took full control of Karantina, and Arafat addressing the Arab Ambassadors in Beirut said that, 'he could no longer be held responsible for the ensuing conduct of Palestinian forces under his command', while Radio Israel reported that PLA troops moved into Lebanon across its borders with Syria. Two days later, the town of Damour and Sadiyyat fell into the hands of the left-wing forces and the PLA.[21] At this point the balance seemed to tilt in favour of the progressive forces. However, the Syrians immediately took the initiative and tried to find ways of creating a stalemate between the warring camps and prevented the formal partition of the country.

Consequently, the third phase in the development of the civil war in Lebanon ensued. It was dominated by the growing military role played by the Syrians and the eventual Arabisation of the Lebanese crisis. At this new level of the conflict, the local forces, Lebanese and Palestinian, were unable to determine the course of events. The conflict was now very much under the control of Syria and to a lesser extent Egypt, Saudi Arabia, Iraq and Libya.

The Syrian Position

For a while the Syrian role in Lebanon appeared to be extremely enigmatic. On the one hand, when the Maronite forces were gaining substantial ground in the fighting, Damascus allowed the PLA to enter Lebanon and check their advance. This was quite understandable in view of the fact that Syria had consistently supported the PLO since it appeared on the Arab political and military scene. However, what was puzzling was the gradual shift in the Syrian attitude once the Progressive forces, joined by a dissident segment of the Lebanese army under the leadership of Lieutenant Ahmad al-Khatib, moved to the offensive in violation of a Syrian-sponsored cease-fire. At this point the Syrian army intervened in the south, east and north, thus pinning down a large part of the progressive forces to defensive positions and allowed the forces of the Maronite Front not only to storm Tel al-Zaatar camp after a long siege, but also to regain most of the positions they had lost north of Jounieh and in the mountains. The intransigence of the Resistance Movement and its radical allies was further checked by the Syrian assault on their positions in Hammana and Bhamdoun and the encirclement of Alley where the mountain headquarters of the Progressive-Palestinian forces was located. By the time the Arab leaders were ready to go to the Ruyadh mini-summit, the PLO and its Lebanese allies had militarily been cut down to size.

There were a number of factors which led to the development of such a situation. One important factor was the sudden growth of the military capabilities of the Progressive Bloc, when towards the end of January, al-Khatib and a group of Muslim officers in the Beqa'a and Akkar districts deserted to the side of the left and formed the Lebanese Arab Army. A couple of weeks later it was revealed that PLA troops of the Ain-Jalut unit had been transferred from Egypt to Lebanon. The latter move was a clear indication that Egypt, together with some other Arab countries especially Iraq, was ready to offer the PLO substantial military assistance to counter the military and political monopoly which Syria sought to exercise over the Palestinian Resistance and the Lebanese crisis. Furthermore Egypt pledged its full support to the PLO and called for an Arab summit to resolve the conflict, while Sadat, in an interview with the Saudi daily *Ukaz* of 21 February, warned the Palestinians against accepting a Syrian tutelage over them. Simultaneously, the Progressive Bloc as well as the Muslim traditional leadership was highly dissatisfied with the terms of the Syrian-sponsored constitutional declaration made by Franjieh in mid-February. All these factors combined tended to encourage the Progressive forces towards the end of February to violate the cease-fire and launch an offensive against the Maronite forces. By 13 March, al-Khatib's troops had occupied all army garrisons in the south, three in the north and several in Beirut; in effect three-quarters of all army positions. Ten days later, the Progressive forces dislodged the Phalange from the seaside hotels in Beirut, and on 25 March, Franjieh fled the presidential palace in Baabda and took refuge in the Maronite district. The leftist forces then advanced on the Christian strongholds in Mount Lebanon in an attempt to penetrate into the heart of the Maronite area. The Syrians, however, were in no mood to tolerate the gradual loss of their control over the situation to the Progressive camp and other Arab governments.

Signs of Syrian dissatisfaction with the PLO had already appeared earlier in the year when Arafat refused to yield to Syrian pressure exercised upon him to enter as a junior partner in an alliance with Syria and Jordan. A spokesman of the PLO announced that his organisation had little to gain from Syria's attempt to revive a PLO presence in Jordan in return for that alliance.[22] On 22 February, Abu Ayad, the second man in Fateh in an interview with the *Financial Times* described the leaders of the pro-Syrian Saiqa Organisation as 'Syrian employees-not-Palestinian leaders'.

As the relationship between the Syrian regime and the Progressive Bloc continued to deteriorate, the Syrians moved to take a more aggressive stand. Early in April, Syrian troops crossed into Lebanon and occupied the border post of al-Masnaa and disarmed al-Khatib's troops who had held the post since February. A Syrian official statement issued on 1 April, warned Junblat and his left-wing supporters that Syria would hold them 'responsible before history for the results of their conduct, particularly for partition, which could be considered the greatest crime committed against the Arab nation and against Lebanon and its people'.[23]

In mid-April a new attempt was made to reconcile the differences between the PLO and the Syrian government, but failed to produce any positive results. In the meantime fighting continued to escalate in Lebanon. Towards the end of May, co-ordinated military moves between the Syrians and the Maronite forces on all fronts were more than obvious. And by the first week of June, the Syrians had blockaded all roads leading to the Muslim quarter of Beirut with the exception of the southern route.

Encouraged by the turn of events the Phalange forces again laid siege to Tel al-Zaatar camp. The camp fell in late August after thirty-five days of a heroic and long struggle. Apart from holding on to some positions in the mountains, the Progressive Bloc seemed to be bent on withdrawing its forces to the main towns on the coast notably Beirut, Saida,

Tyre and Tripoli. Militarily, a final show-down with the Syrians was expected to take place in the towns. The Syrians, sensing the great difficulty and perhaps the huge cost of getting involved in an urban guerilla warfare, preferred to mark time, and opted for a political solution which eventually yielded the same results. The summit meeting in Riyadh held on 16 October, offered them this opportunity.

It would seem that the Syrian position in Lebanon had been largely determined by two major considerations stemming from Syrian national interests. Firstly, the Syrian policy-maker was determined not to allow the situation in Lebanon to drift into the actual partitioning of the country into a separate Muslim and a Christian state. Secondly, Syria was keen, once and for all, to control the Palestinian presence in Lebanon and establish its hegemony over a region extending to Beirut and possibly Amman.

From a Syrian point of view, a partitioned Lebanon would have partly meant the emergence of a political entity on Syria's borders which was Muslim-Palestinian, radical and certainly more inclined towards a continuous confrontation with Israel. Such a situation would have left the initiative of war and peace in the region in the hands of the new Lebanese state and Israel. It would have also posed a number of critical questions to the Syrian policy-maker for which he had to find answers. What would the Syrian position have been if in the course of the confrontation Israel decided to occupy southern Lebanon? In such a case Syria's alternatives would have been either to face the Israelis or sit quietly and lose face. In any case, the initiative would have been left entirely outside Syria's political will. At the same time the emergence of a purely Christian state in Mount Lebanon would have carried with it, in the long run, the potential of another Israel being created in the region. Close co-operation and co-ordination might then have ensued between the Christian and Jewish states, and Syria's future and its existence might then have been endangered. With such disastrous prospects in mind, the Syrians moved on two occasions to prevent the virtual partitioning of Lebanon. The first time was in January 1976, when the Maronite forces appeared to gain the upper hand in the fighting, and the second time was in April after the Progressive Bloc had launched its offensive. In the first instance, the Foreign Minister of Syria threatened that if need be his government would take over Lebanon. In the second instance, Syria went beyond mere threats to deploy its own armed forces against those of the Palestinian Resistance and the Progressive Bloc. In Riyadh, Assad was at pains to point out to other Arab heads of states that Syria 'backed the Palestinians in Lebanon when they faced liquidation. We stood against them when it became a question of partition'.[24]

The ideal situation for the Syrians in Lebanon was that of redressing the balance between the two fighting camps, and bringing about a compromise which would preserve the unity of the country. Within this context, Syria kept the channels of negotiations open with the two competing parties and made every effort to achieve a settlement. The last of these efforts was the seventeen-point constitutional declaration which in essence, except for minor modifications, tended to revive the old sectarian system, but failed to satisfy the demands of the Progressive Bloc. However, as the Progressive forces continued to take an intransigent position, the Syrians stepped in. The moment then had arrived for an Arab summit, lest that other Arab countries might throw their military weight behind one faction or the other. It was rumoured at the time that Cairo was entertaining the thought of dispatching Egyptian troops to Lebanon.

Syria's initiatives in Lebanon were not only geared to preventing partition, but also sought to strengthen Syria's position in the region as a whole. For many years Syria had been closely co-operating with the PLO on the account of its own relationships with other Arab countries in the area, notably Jordan. It would seem that after the second Sinai agreement, the Syrian and Jordanian regimes found themselves in a position of relative isolation. Assad accused Kissinger of dividing the Arabs, while the Jordanian Prime Minister refused to support the Sinai agreement publicly. 'Assad all but described Kissinger as Israel's foreign minister: Hussein warned me [Sheehan] of "new disasters not far away" '[25] Both countries felt that a joint effort was needed and that a common front might lead to extracting better terms from the Americans in future negotiations. In December 1975, co-operation between the two regimes had reached a point of conducting joint military manoeuvres to test the Syrian defences against a simulated Israeli attack on Damascus. Some ten thousand Jordanian troops took part in the manoeuvres. Throughout 1976, visits were regularly exchanged

between the two heads of state, and top ranking officials in both
governments met often to work out joint military and political plans.
In the meantime, Assad attempted to draw the PLO into his alliance
with Hussein but without much luck. He probably figured out that with
a docile Palestinian partner on his side his hand would be strengthened
in any future negotiations at Geneva. But time was still on his side, the
American elections were to be held in early November and before that
no peace initiative was expected. However, as time passed, he began to
stack his cards for a final count. The Syrian circle was completed in
October 1976, a few weeks before the American elections. The Riyadh
mini-summit, held in mid-October and attended by Syria, Egypt, Saudi
Arabia, Kuwait, Lebanon and the PLO, did not only endorse the Syrian
military campaign in Lebanon but went a step further. It provided an
Arab political cover for Syria's action and pledged financial support
for its military intervention in Lebanon under the guise of an 'Arab
deterrent force'.

Other Arab Regimes Fall in Line

The Riyadh mini-summit satisfied in different ways other Arab regimes.
In return for a Syrian free hand in Lebanon, Egypt had some important
gains to make. Both Syria and the PLO were now in no position to
accuse Egypt of betraying the 'Arab sacred cause' for its acceptance of
the second Sinai agreement. Internally, at least, and as far as Egyptian
public opinion was concerned, Sadat emerged as the maker of peace in
Lebanon and the saviour of the Palestinian people. Finally, with the
prospect of a new peace initiative in the Middle East, Egypt preserved
the Palestinian card at its disposal and the disposal of other Arab governments including Syria and Jordan. As for Saudi Arabia and Kuwait, the
PLO in the last few years had become an embarrassment to such Arab
governments. On the one hand, seeking to play the major role in Arab
politics, Saudi Arabia found herself in a position which required her to
act as the champion of the Palestinian cause. At the same time, she
recognised that an autonomous Palestinian radical movement might
eventually revolutionise the whole situation in the region and open the
door for communism to enter the Arab world. The left-wing outlook
and the growing association of the Resistance Movement with the
communists and radical forces in Lebanon led to a change of heart on

the part of the Saudis. There were even some claims made by the Palestinian Rejection Front to the effect that Saudi Arabian and other Arab oil-producing countries were providing the Maronite Front with financial aid. What was more obvious was the fact that since the Syrian intervention had begun against the Progressive forces the Saudis had conferred their blessings upon it. The Saudi Minister of State was reported on 26 March to have said that his government 'appreciated the efforts of the Syrian leaders to re-establish security in Lebanon'.[26]

It would seem that Saudi Arabia and Kuwait had throughout the Lebanese crisis been interested in accomplishing two main objectives. Firstly, they were interested in curbing the revolutionary zeal of the Resistance Movement so as to render it more acquiescent to Arab pressure. This could have been achieved only by allowing Syria enough time as well as affording her political and perhaps financial support to contain the Resistance Movement. Secondly, both countries moved at the right moment to bring about an Arab consensus, especially between Egypt and Syria. Once the first objective, containment, was achieved Riyadh was ready to receive the Arab heads of state in a mini-summit to achieve the second objective, namely an Arab disengagement in Lebanon. Out of all the Arab regimes only Libya and Iraq refused to endorse the agreement reached in Riyadh. Both countries had since the eruption of the civil war pledged their unyielding support to the Progressive forces, but their impact on the development of events in the area compared with that of Syria, Saudi Arabia and Egypt was marginal.

The Super-Powers

A complete picture of the development of the Lebanese conflict and its resolution cannot be drawn without examining briefly the political position held by the two super-powers. To what extent were the Americans and the Russians involved in the crisis? Late in 1975, the French special envoy to Beirut, Couve de Merville found it difficult to comment on such a question, 'because it is evidently difficult to define their game for the time being'.[27] A year later it was still difficult to ascertain the level of their direct involvement; however, it was possible to make some reasonable suggestions concerning their political stands towards the development of events in the area. One question which was raised was this: in a conflict which dragged on for over eighteen months and in which all kinds of weapons were used including heavy artillery, tanks, rockets, etc. . . . who provided this inexhaustible mine of ammunition? There were indications that some of it was bought on the international arms market, some was acquired from the Lebanese army as it disintegrated into small factions, certainly some Arab governments and Israel made their contributions to one side or the other, but to sustain such an inflow of arms and ammunition for such a long period of time required some sort of involvement by the super-powers. Some sources estimated that in the last year of fighting there was on average something like half a million dollars being expended daily in the form of firepower. Could the Arab governments collectively dispense with such an amount of ammunition without jeopardising their own defences? But perhaps this is a question for the military expert to consider before a final conclusion can be reached. Politically, however, some answers might be discerned.

As the crisis unfolded, the USA gradually took a more sympathetic attitude towards the Syrian military intervention in Lebanon. At first when the PLO forces entered Lebanon on the side of the Progressive forces in early January 1976, a State Department spokesman warned that the USA was opposed to any outside intervention by any country including Syria and Israel.[28] But towards the end of the same month, the USA commended Syria for its 'constructive role' in arranging a ceasefire between the two opposing forces.[29] On 30 March, and as the Syrian troops began to harass the Progressive forces, the State Department maintained its opposition to foreign intervention, but again praised Syria's 'peace efforts'.[30] At the same time, Dean Brown who arrived in Lebanon on a fact-finding mission adopted the Syrian stand on its opposition to partition. He stressed Washington's disapproval of any action which might lead to partition.[31] Finally, three weeks later, a White House spokesman announced that President Ford had ended his opposition to outside military intervention and approved Syria's action in Lebanon.[32] From then on the Syrian role in Lebanon continued to enjoy the blessings of the USA.

Whether Syria had informed the USA of its intentions in Lebanon or not was questionable, but what was quite clear was that the Syrians had played consciously or unconsciously into the hands of the Ameri-

cans. Nothing could have pleased the American and Israeli policy-
makers more than the thought of facing in the future at the negotiating
table a weakened and tamed Palestinian national movement, surviving
under the suffocating wings of the Arab governments, and perhaps
even represented by one of these governments, possibly Jordan.

Since 1972, the Russians had been finding it increasingly difficult
to maintain a foothold in the area. Once Egypt was lost to the Americans, the Soviet Union tended to pin its hopes on Iraq, Libya, the PLO
and, last but not least, Syria. However, the Russian position was further
eroded as a result of the conflicts which occurred among its Arab allies.
Iraq and the PLO stood on one side in the Lebanese crisis while Syria
joined the opposing camp and drifted into a policy of near collusion
with the USA. The Soviet Union, in an effort to rectify the situation,
exerted some pressure on the Syrians, but to no avail. The political
spokesman of the PLO emphasised that the Soviet Union had throughout the crisis supported the Palestinian Resistance in every possible
material, moral, and political way. Furthermore Soviet leaders adam-
antly opposed the military intervention of the Syrians in the Beqa'a
valley early in June, and refused to issue, at the end of Khaddam's
visit to Moscow in the summer of 1976, a joint communique endorsing
the Syrian moves. On 9 June, Brezhnev addressed a letter to President
Assad in which he expressed his strong objections to the Syrian action
in Lebanon.[33] At a later date, Assad complained to the Arab heads of
state in Riyadh that 'The Soviet Union now blame us for preventing
the establishment of a leftist state in Lebanon'[34] At no point during the
course of the conflict in Lebanon did the Resistance Movement com-
plain of a shortage in Russian-made firearms or ammunition. This perhaps prompted the leaders of the Phalange Party to reiterate on almost
every occasion their concern at what they believed to be a plot against
Lebanon designed by international communism. In fact what the
Russians were trying to do was to maintain their foothold in the region
against what looked to them to be an American attempt to oust them.

Conclusion

The outcome of the civil war in Lebanon benefited at every level one
side in the conflict to the exclusion of the other. On the international
level the Russians seemed to suffer a serious set-back in the region as a

whole and in Syria in particular. On the Arab level, the Arab regimes managed, perhaps for a long time to come, to impose their will on the Palestinian Resistance and its leftist allies. On the Lebanese level, the position of the Maronite Front and more notably the Phalange Party had been consolidated, while that of the Progressive Bloc was greatly undermined. Israel stood to gain from the erosion of the position of the left in Lebanon, the containment of the Resistance Movement, the growing influence of moderate Arab regimes seeking a peaceful settlement at the hands of the USA, and the relative revival of American hegemony in the Middle East.

The tragic events which engulfed Lebanon for one year and a half do not make much sense unless an attempt is made to examine their repercussions on the evolution of a new, more stable system of government, and the achievement of an over-all solution to the Arab-Israeli conflict. There is no desire here to suggest that there was a conspiracy behind the crisis, although such a conclusion had not been excluded by the participants in the conflict. However, it is reasonable to assert that the recent events in the region prepared the grounds for two probable major developments.

Firstly, a new political order is being established in Lebanon to replace the old system which, on at least two occasions in the modern history of the country, proved to be most fragile and inadequate. It is well-known that the new President of Lebanon, Elias Sarkis was one of Shehab's most faithful disciples. In 1970, he contested the presidency against Franjieh, but the latter won by a majority of one vote, and as a result political feudalism or the Zeims system of government made a come-back to power. From 1958 to 1970, Shehabism represented a new trend in Lebanese politics. It was a serious attempt to displace the old power structure based on sectarianism by building up a strong central government and a tight internal security system.

Shehabism had tried to institute checks upon the operations of civil relations in order to make the state the sole political unit in the country. Its Deuxieme Bureau was supposed to displace the traditional Chieftains by taking over their role as the sole Za'im from whom state benefits would be obtained. In pursuit of this policy the Deuxième Bureau promoted the rise in the Sunni areas of more or less popular leaderships who capitalised on their role in the 1958 civil war and who were outside the control of traditional leaders.[35]

Today Sarkis has a better chance than his predecessors Helou and Shehab to realise the Shehabist model. He comes to power as the saviour of the country after it had been torn apart by a devastating internal strife. He has the political, military and financial backing of the Arab governments which initiated the Riyadh agreement. His task is further facilitated by the fact that the civil war had discredited the traditional opponents of Shehabism, namely the old sectarian leaders. On the Muslim side a new political leadership has emerged, while on the Christian side the position of the Phalange Party has become predominant. In the future Lebanon might witness the gradual disappearance of such well-known figures as the As'ad, Salam, Yafi and even Shamoun and Franjieh. Instead, the newly emerging regime might depend on the younger generation of Muslim and Christian leaders who made a name for themselves on the battle-field in the recent civil war. The gap between the new Muslim leadership and the Phalange might prove to be not as wide as had first been expected. Bashir Jumayyil, commander of the Phalange forces has recently stressed that Lebanon could never return to the old arrangement, 'we do not want to revive the 1943 pact'. He urged for the establishment of a new secular Lebanon with a strong central government. His brother, Amin, claimed that the Party had fought in essence against sectarianism, feudalism and those who regarded parts of Lebanon as their personal fiefs.[36]

In the absence of a Palestinian military presence a compromise between the Progressive Bloc and the Phalange might be feasible, especially under a Shehabist form of government. But with the rise of 'neo-Shehabism' Lebanon's 'sectarian democracy' would become the sacrifice. Instead, an Arabised Lebanon might emerge in which the state plays a major political and stabilising role, similar to that played by central governments in other parts of the Arab world.

Secondly, the Palestinian Resistance has undoubtedly suffered a serious military set-back. Its military presence in Lebanon, the last sanctuary for Palestinian armed struggle has been greatly undermined.

Even its political existence has been placed at the mercy of Arab governments. Such a change in the fortunes of the Resistance Movement has eliminated an embarrassing challenge to the sovereignty and political interests of some Arab countries. Over and above this, the military decline of the Movement has removed the threat of radicalising the political and social conditions of some Arab societies. The organic links between the Palestinian Resistance and the Lebanese left have accordingly been dismantled. Recognising the facts of the new situation, a prominent leader of the Lebanese left in a joint meeting with the PLO said, 'From now on we have to tackle the Lebanese issues . . . As for the Resistance you should concentrate on the Cairo Agreement and its implementation.'[37] In other words, the Progressive Bloc was absolving the Resistance Movement from its previous commitments to the left.

Arab governments appear to be under the impression that the year 1977 might witness a final settlement to the Arab-Israeli conflict in Geneva. Awaiting such an eventuality the Palestinian Resistance is to remain within the confines drawn by the Arab regimes, and overbidding on the part of the PLO would not be tolerated. The solution envisaged for the Palestinians is that of a West Bank-Gaza state. This is the nearest one could translate the often-repeated formula made by Arab statesmen regarding 'the national rights of the Palestinians'. The Syrian-Arab military intervention in Lebanon brought home to the Palestinians, under the present conditions of the Arab world, the impossibility of taking an independent stand from that of the Arab regimes. Accordingly, the political spokesman of the Resistance Movement declared at the UN last November that his organisation was willing to go to Geneva and accept a Palestinian state in the West Bank and Gaza.[38]

However, while this looks to be the most likely path the Palestinians might follow, it is not yet certain whether other options have been entirely closed or not. After all, many observers believed in late 1970, after the collapse of the Resistance Movement in Amman, that for all intents and purposes the efforts of the Palestinian organisations had come to an end. Nevertheless, the Resistance Movement eventually managed to exploit the differences among the Arab countries and gradually succeeded in gaining a political and military foothold in Lebanon. While the Arab party seems to be well prepared to go to

Geneva today, other parties are under no such pressure to do likewise. And even if a Geneva conference ultimately materialised, there is no guarantee that the Arab side would be able to extract the demands it has put forward: a Palestinian state and an Israeli withdrawal to the 1967 borders.

The road to Geneva might prove to be too long and difficult. In the meantime, the Arab regimes cannot guarantee their own stability at home nor can they sustain a common front for ever. If for one reason or another inter-Arab conflict is again intensified, or if any of the front-line regimes undergoes a radical change, the Resistance Movement might once more be presented with a golden opportunity to revive itself politically and militarily. And this is neither speculation nor wishful thinking. In a region such as the Arab world political and military variables often elude the sharp senses of the political analyst.

January 1977

Notes

1. E.A. Salem, *Modernization Without Revolution: Lebanon's Experience*, Indiana University Press, Bloomington and London, 1973, p. 4.

2. As quoted in K.S. Salibi, *The Modern History of Lebanon*, London, 1965, p. 187.

3. Since 1932, Lebanon has had no population census. It is, however, widely believed that the Shi'is form the largest single sect. It is estimated that together with their co-religionists, the Sunnis, they comprise some 60 per cent of Lebanon's population.

4. Salem, p. 45.

5. *Al-Nahar*, 8 July 1975.

6. Ibid., 9 July 1975.

7. Ibid., 10 July 1975.

8. Ibid., 22 August 1976.

9. Eric Rouleau, *Le Monde*, 20-25 September 1975.

10. W. Quandt, F. Jabber, A.M. Lesch, *The Politics of Palestinian Nationalism*, University of California Press, 1973, p. 193.

11. *Al-Hawadith*, Beirut, 24 October 1975.

12. N. Howard, *Current History*, January 1976, p. 6.

13. Salem, p. 15.

14. *Al-Amal*, 1 August 1975, p. 5.

15. M. Johnson, 'Confessionalism and Individualism in Lebanon', *Review of Middle East Studies I*, London, 1975, p. 87.

16. Ibid., p. 88.

17. H. Mandis, *Labour and Labourers in the Palestinian Camp: A Field-Study in Tel al-Zaatar Camp*, (Arabic), Beirut, 1974, p. 25.

18. A. Hourani, 'Ideologies of the Mountain and the City', *Essays on the Crisis in Lebanon* (ed. Roger Owen), London, 1976, p. 37.

19. T. Khalaf, 'The Phalange and the Maronite Community: From Lebanonism to Marotinism', *Essays . . .*, p. 46.

20. *Al-Nahar*, 22 August 1975.

21. *Arab Report and Record*, no. 2, 16-31 January 1976.

22. *Al-Sayyad*, Beirut, 25 February 1976.

23. *Arab Report and Record*, no. 7, 1-15 April 1976.

24. *Events*, no. 3, Beirut, 5 November 1976, p. 19.

25. E.R.F. Sheehan, 'How Kissinger Did It', *Foreign Policy*, Spring 1975, p. 65.

26. *Arab Report and Record*, no. 6, 16-31 March 1976.

27. *L'Orient-Le Jour*, Beirut, 25 November 1975.

28. *Arab Report and Record*, no. 1, 1-15 January 1976.

29. Ibid., no. 2, 16-31 January 1976.

30. Ibid., no. 6, 16-31 March 1976.

31. Ibid., no. 7, 1-15 April 1976.

32. Ibid., no.8, 16-30 April 1976.

33. *Tali'a*, Cairo, October 1976, p. 62.

34. *Events*, p. 19.

35. A. Al-Azmeh, 'The Progressive Forces', *Essays . . .*, p. 63.

36. *Al-Sayyad*, 18 November 1976.

37. Ibid., 11 November 1976.

38. *Al-Hawadith*, 26 November 1976.

3 PROSPECTS OF WAR AND PEACE IN THE MIDDLE EAST

The recent civil war in Lebanon has weakened the military and political standing of the Palestinian Resistance Movement (PRM) and undermined the revolutionary potential which it once enjoyed. As a matter of fact, and to be more precise, certain changes have taken place in the Arab world since October 1973 which renders the position of the PLO as well as the Arab left less viable than before. A new situation has been created. It is characterised by the political and military dominance of a coalition of Arab countries consisting of the front-line regimes and the oil-producing countries in the Arab Peninsula.[1]

For some time now, observers of the Arab scene have noticed that on the whole the level of co-ordination among the Arab regimes has improved tremendously since 1973. There were moments when disagreements, especially between Syria and Egypt, seemed to disrupt the newly established climate of Arab consensus, but these were soon overcome through the mediation of the other regimes concerned and did not last long enough to produce any damaging effects. Official Arab consensus and understanding appeared to operate not only in the direction of improving the bargaining position of the Arab governments *vis-à-vis* Israel and the USA, but also internally, tending to strengthen the hold of these governments over their own peoples and the PRM. In this respect much has been accomplished.

Firstly, the Arab regimes have managed through the use of Syrian military power and Saudi financial assistance to bring about the military subordination of the Palestinian forces in Lebanon. Today, the armed presence of the Palestinians is confined to two areas in Lebanon; one in Beirut and the other in the south. However, more important is the fact that while the PLO is allowed to control some of the refugee camps in and around Beirut, the Syrian forces under the guise of the so-called Arab deterrent force have deployed their heavy artillery and tanks around the Palestinian positions, thus threatening to eliminate the last strongholds of the PLO. In southern Lebanon, the Resistance

67

Movement is bogged down in a futile battle imposed upon it by the Lebanese Christian Bloc and the Israeli army. But the Arab regimes have not yet moved in to a kill. At this point, and before a final settlement of the Middle East conflict is reached, the Arab regimes seem to be more inclined to preserve the Palestinian card in the hope of acquiring in future negotiations with Israel, parts of the territories they had lost in 1967. If the Arab onslaught on the PRM has stopped short of destroying it, it did so simply to allow the USA enough time to work out a satisfactory agreement between the Arab governments and Israel.

Secondly, the Arab regimes have managed during the last few years to subordinate the PRM politically. More recently pressure has been brought to bear on the PLO to co-operate with the Jordanian regime, a step towards the final incorporation of whatever Palestinian entity emerges in the future into the wider framework of the Jordanian state. A solution on these lines seems to allay the fears and objections of Israel concerning an independent Palestinian entity and appears to keep the Palestinians under Arab control so as not to disturb the stability of the region.

Further evidence of Arab official solidarity is seen in the forging of economic links among the Arab states with the exception of a few of them, notably Iraq and Libya. The purpose of economic co-operation is twofold. On the one hand, it helps to bring a measure of social and economic stability to the front-line Arab countries, where the social and economic fabric of society is almost on the verge of collapse. Nothing could be more interesting than watching the Arab oil-producing countries in the Peninsula rushing to save the Egyptian regime from the severe crisis it faced during the food riots in early 1977. There seems to be a growing awareness among the Arab regimes of the fact that, if for any reason one of them falls, the rest will face a similar fate in the future. On the other hand, the chain of Arab official solidarity has to be consolidated against the radical forces in the area and more particularly Palestinian insurgency. The Riyadh mini-summit in late 1976 was a step in this direction, whereby Arab differences were ironed out at the expense of the PLO. This was followed by the numerous exchanges of visits between Arab heads of state, ministers of foreign affairs and ministers of economy to work out the details of a more viable front against the threatening impact of the deteriorating economic situation.

Arab official co-operation is further enhanced by the joint ventures established among the Arab governments, semi-official institutions and private entrepreneurs in the Arab countries. The Arab Board of War Industries which was launched in early 1977 tended to cement the personal as well as the professional links among the Arab army officers. One of its purposes is to provide an atmosphere of understanding among them to assist in maintaining some of the Arab ruling elites in power in times of crisis. On two recent occasions, Numeiri's regime in Sudan owed its continued existence to military aid from one of the Arab neighbouring countries. Simultaneously, economic support in the form of gifts and loans are regularly pumped into the bankrupt economies of the front-line countries to enable them to overcome internal upheavals. Arab funds generated by donations from the oil-producing countries are established to subsidise economic projects by way of consolidating the positions of the Arab ruling elites. Even a large segment of the Arab intelligentsia including intellectuals, journalists, experts and many economists are being co-opted by the Arab regimes to help project a better image of the Arab leadership. In recent years an Arab transnational bourgeois class has gradually developed, acting on behalf of the men in power and providing them with technical know-how, advice, and an intellectual and legal cover for their ever-growing appetite for consumption.

The suppression of the radical impulse in the Arab world has not stopped at the political and military levels but extends to include the intellectual level too. In this context, a siege on Arab intellectual activity has been imposed. *Dirasat Arabiyya*, one of the leading monthlies in Beirut now requires not only the approval of the Lebanese censor but also the agreement of a Syrian censor who co-ordinates with his Egyptian counterpart. While at one time the Lebanese press enjoyed a large measure of freedom, today it is stifled by restrictions of all sorts imposed upon it by a tight system of censorship. As a result, the Lebanese press has become as dull and misleading as any of the semi-official papers published in Arab capitals. At the same time Arab journalists of a radical tendency are being laid off and in some cases arrested and put in prison, while their newspapers and journals are shut down.

Today, the forces of counter-revolution in the Arab world seem to be in full swing. Before 1973, these forces were frequently acting separately and in a contradictory fashion; cohesion was lacking and instead conflict was the prominent feature of the relationship between the Arab governments. However, since 1973 serious attempts have been made firstly to iron out the differences among the Arab rulers and secondly to eliminate the potential political and social threat posed by the radical forces against them. Pan-Arabism has after all made some strides forward, but the irony of the situation is that it is confined only to governments and some interest groups. The Arab peoples, the Palestinians included, are the victims of this new trend of pan-Arabism. The two worlds of the Arabs have never been as clearly defined and separate as they are now; the world of abundance and the world of poverty, the haves and have-nots, the mighty and powerful and the frustrated and crushed — two worlds which may at any time violently clash and disrupt the façade of relative stability which Arab governments display before the other nations.

To guarantee their newly acquired solidarity and power, the Arab regimes sought an alliance with the USA. Persuading themselves of the naïve idea that the USA holds in its own hands all the cards pertaining to the Arab-Israeli conflict, they eventually fell into line with its wider military and political strategy in the area. From the time that Egypt expelled the Russian experts in 1972 to the time it intervened militarily, together with Morocco, on behalf of Mobutu's regime in Zaire, the general tendency of the Arab official bloc has been to play unnecessarily into the hands of the American strategists. This whole-hearted support for American policy in Africa and Asia has driven some Arab governments to act as the local policemen for the USA interests in the region. It is true that they are doing so partly to guard themselves against neighbouring regimes which appear to take a more radical stance on internal and foreign policy issues, but the main objective is the expectation that such enthusiasm for American policy should pay off in the near future. The USA is expected to initiate by the end of 1977 a peace process by which the following is to be achieved:

1. Enough American pressure on Israel to force it to move to a slightly modified position from that which it held on the eve of the June war in 1967.

2. A political arrangement to accommodate the Palestinians on the lines of a West Bank-Gaza solution linked to Jordan.

3. In the long run, Arab regimes such as Egypt and Syria expect enough American aid and Arab financial assistance to flow in their direction so as to sustain themselves politically and economically.

The Arab plan for peace in the Middle East seems to assume two interrelated things; an American ability to exert the sort of pressure needed on Israel and an American willingness to make use of it. There is some evidence to show that, while the USA is not as confident as the Arab regimes are, concerning its own influence on Israel, yet it is clear enough that the USA is willing to use whatever persuasive methods it has on hand to reach a mutually satisfactory arrangement. It would seem that the recent changes in the Arab world have led the USA to recognise that it has more to gain from its rapport with the Arabs than from its persistent and uncritical support to Israel. The oil is perhaps one factor which may have worked towards such a change in American attitudes. However, in a wider political context, it appears that the collapse of Nasserism in 1967 and with it the sudden retreat of the movement of Arab nationalism and Arab socialism, culminating in the growing dominance of Arab moderation, offered the USA an opportunity to play a more active role in the region. The Arab regimes today are not divided as they used to be into reactionary and progressive regimes, and those Arab leaders who have met Carter and, before him, Ford and Nixon, appear to be from an American stance wise, reasonable, understanding and gracious. Unlike the fiery and extremist 'demagogues' of the past, the new Arab leadership is a sensible and a reliable ally with an even temperament which does not lend itself to ideas such as nationalism, socialism or communism. The need for an Israel to act as the local policeman against over-ambitious and revolutionary Arab schemes has been undermined. The new allies are modest in their demands, very accommodating to American advice and efficient at performing their counter-revolutionary task. In such a short period of time since 1973 they have proved to be better placed than Israel in suppressing the PRM and containing Soviet influence in the Middle East and Africa. Naturally in the absence of Arab insurgency, the USA is more inclined to see to it that none of its Arab allies is put in an embarrassing situation. On the contrary, it is expected that a serious effort will be made to extend a helping hand in the form of economic aid and reasonable concessions from Israel to those Arab regimes which are lacking in political and economic stability. The Geneva Conference is one such step in the direction of stabilising the fragile situation in the Middle East. On it depends the survival of some Arab governments, without it their presence becomes questionable. And if that is the case, then we should be talking about an entirely different Middle East scenario.

However, before examining other prospects for the future development of the Middle East we ought to consider yet another factor which tends to reinforce the conditions acting in favour of a settlement as proposed by the Arab regimes.

It has been observed that, while the Arab regimes have been closing their ranks, the radical camp including the PRM has been suffering from internal organisational and ideological dissension. The seeds of discord appeared soon after the June war, when different Arab governments sponsored a number of Palestinian armed groups. In 1970, following the defeat of the PRM in Jordan, radical Arab movements began to review the situation more critically. Some Arab leftists, among them Sadeq al-Azm, severely criticised the PRM and focused on its inability to transform itself into a Marxist-Leninist movement and its failure to gain the organised support of the Arab and Palestinian masses. He condemned the movement's lack of understanding of the basic contradictions existing between it and the Arab regimes, its compromising attitude towards the Jordanian regime before September 1970, its ideological confusion and its petty bourgeois outlook. In the final analysis the PRM is seen as a product of the Arab political and social set-up, suffering from the same defects which Arab petty bourgeois regimes have suffered from; namely the inability of these regimes to confront imperialism and Israel, their indecisive attitude in resolving social and economic contradictions internally and finally their unconditional surrender to the Arab reactionary regimes under the hegemony of the USA. In other words, the Arabs have not been able to produce a genuine revolutionary movement, but a Palestinian version of the rise of the Arab middle classes to power in some Arab countries. The critical approach of al-Azm and other leftists is looked upon as a healthy sign within the ranks of the revolutionary camp.

The total effect of the factors outlined above, the growing solidarity among the Arab ruling elites, the backing afforded by the USA to the Arab official bloc, and finally the increasing signs of disintegration among Arab radicals and the PRM, tend to strengthen the initiative proposed by the Arabs for a settlement. However, time, the social and political nature of the Arab regimes, and Israel's over-confidence in its military capabilities may prove to be insurmountable obstacles to the realisation of a peace settlement.

While a number of obstacles can be detected concerning the conclusion of a final peace settlement in the Middle East, one of the most important is that which pertains to the creation of a Palestinian state. It is envisaged that the new Palestinian entity will include the West Bank and Gaza linked to Jordan. At the basis of this suggestion is an assumption that a displaced community may eventually agree to live under a wider political framework once it is provided with a territorial base, reasonable sources of income and a measure of political and cultural autonomy. There are a number of cases in European and North American history where such arrangements have worked. A solution of this kind has frequently achieved a measure of success where the level of political and administrative decentralisation is relatively high. In the Arab world minority groups, displaced communities and even individuals are stifled by the growing trend of centralisation. It is as though these societies are set on a path characterised by highly centralised systems of government. Over and over again the Arab peoples are promised by one regime after another that they will soon enjoy the benefits of democracy, when all the time measures are being implemented to concentrate enormous powers in the hands of the top leadership. Behind the neatly designed constitutions of the Arab regimes hides the ugly face of dictatorship, oppression and the police state. Without exaggeration, the Arab world has never witnessed in this century such a wave of suppression and violation of human rights as it is encountering today. The Arab regimes have recently exploited all the modern means of mass media to hide the crimes they are committing against their own people.

A Palestinian state linked to Jordan is another way of saying the subordination of the Palestinian people to the Jordanian monarch. Of this neither the Palestinians nor the Jordanian regime have any doubt. If an attempt is made at Geneva to establish a genuine federation or confederation between the proposed new Palestinian state and Jordan, then neither King Hussein nor any of the Arab leaders will be interested in the subject. As a matter of fact the Jordanian government would not even know how to handle such a proposal. It is so alien to the nature and values of the Arab ruling classes that the issue may not even appear on the agenda. What will certainly be discussed are the safeguards which would ensure the subjection of the new state to a joint Arab-Israeli control. Already some other Arab leaders, let alone King Hussein, have expressed their serious concern regarding the PLO position on the issue. According to *The Times*, Sadat at a press conference held on the eve of Mr Vance's arrival in Cairo, 'agreed tonight that he and Mr Arafat differed over the prospective links between a new Palestinian state and Jordan. He wants to see such links in existence before a state is created and Mr Arafat wants to deal with the problem afterwards.'[2] The PLO may have to be coerced into accepting the conditions dictated in Geneva, but in the long run the resentment of the Palestinians will remain and may take an active form once the situation changes in the Arab countries. Palestinian resentment may also play into the hands of some Arab regimes if they choose to disrupt the existing spirit of Arab accord. At the moment, the Syrians seem to be less sympathetic than Sadat to the idea of a linkage between Jordan and the proposed Palestinian state. President Assad may prefer the new Palestinian entity to be more closely linked to Syria than to Jordan. However, it is still too early to elaborate on this particular point. It is sufficient to point out that, with a proposal such as the one entertained by the Arab governments, the Palestinian problem will continue to be an explosive issue. In spite of the lip-service paid by the Arab leaders to the Palestinian cause which they often claim is at the root of the Arab-Israeli conflict, the truth of the matter is that the Arab regimes are going to Geneva to settle once and for all their differences with Israel. The Palestinians may again be sacrificed to Arab official interests, but the problem of a displaced community will remain, haunting the stability of the Arab regimes and threatening to erupt every now and then, just as the Kurdish question has haunted every Iraqi regime since the establishment of the modern state of Iraq.

Palestinian insurgency under the present political circumstances is not an immediate threat to the Arab plans for peace in the Middle East. However, what could damage the prospects for a settlement is a sudden change of regime in one of the front-line Arab countries, or a state of civil strife which may hamper the implementation of vital political decisions. It is possible that the drive for a peaceful settlement may be reversed. If for example the Jordanian regime suffers a set-back, which is very unlikely in the near future, then the whole concept of a new Palestinian state will be shattered. What is more probable, however, is a radical change in the political situation of Egypt or Syria where the two regimes seem to be more amenable to political and social instability. Sadat's role in the development of the recent drive for a peaceful settlement in the Middle East is indispensable to the success of the project. He may rightly be called the architect of the Arab quest for peace. He took several daring stands such as committing himself to recognising Israel and establishing normal relationships with her once an agreement is signed. The loss of Sadat would bring the efforts for a peaceful solution to a standstill. On the other hand, the loss of Assad's regime in Damascus would automatically undermine the military restraints imposed on the PRM in Lebanon. Each of the Arab front-line countries plays a distinct and crucial role, complementing one another in the course of achieving a peaceful solution. Egypt takes the political initiative, Syria keeps the PLO under control and Jordan is the framework within which a solution can become operative. Behind them stand the major Arab oil-producing countries sustaining them financially and using oil as a political leverage.

However, such an arrangement cannot last long. The magnitude of the social and economic problems which some of the front-line Arab countries face cannot be solved by donations and gifts from abroad. Despite the fact that some portion of the foreign aid received is being utilised in a productive way, yet most of it is being spent on paying back short-term loans and in many cases it is merely consumed. Apart from the military expenditure, two factors seem to counteract any attempt at the full utilisation of foreign aid. One is the economic conditions attached to such aid and its political implications. The other is the consumption habits which the Arab ruling classes have developed. The food riots in Egypt in January 1977, were triggered off by the insistence of the IMF that the Egyptian government take some unpopular economic measures before further loans were given to Egypt. The short-lived measures suggested by the IMF and implemented by the government may have been economically sound, but the political repercussions could have been much more damaging had the Egyptian government not backed down on them early enough to avoid a catastrophe. It is interesting to note that the relationship between the donors and the recipients of economic aid in the Middle East contains an inherent contradiction. While on the one hand, the rich Arab countries and American-sponsored aid institutions have all the goodwill in the world to maintain the political and economic stability of the Egyptian and Syrian regimes, yet on the other hand, in the process of offering their assistance they tend to tie the hands of those whom they are trying to help. Sometimes, the conditions attached to economic aid extend to the political realm and that in itself is another kind of danger. The Saudis often advise the recipients of financial aid to tolerate the activities of Muslim fanatic groups. This kind of danger has recently been quite obvious in the case of a country like Egypt.

Another perhaps more serious threat to the fabric of some front-line Arab societies is the attitude of the upper classes, including the ruling elite, to consumption. Initially most of these social and political categories came to acquire their wealth during the last three decades. Originally they came from a middle-class social background, which included army officers, technocrats, bureaucrats and members of the liberal professions. At first they were reluctant to take decisive stands on social and economic issues but were more inclined to introduce measures which ultimately destroyed the economic basis of the semi-feudal and capitalist classes. The new ruling elites oscillated between a desire to improve the lot of the poorer classes by implementing land reform laws and creating a public sector after nationalising some industries, and an urge to satisfy their own ambitions as a ruling class by enjoying the benefits accruing to them from controlling power and wealth. Ultimately, they seem to have abandoned their hesitation and plunged themselves, as the old ruling classes used to do, into a process of conspicuous consumption which has added to the depletion of the scarce resources of their societies. Much of the aid they now receive from outside seems to be channelled into buying fancy cars, colour TV sets, and luxury housing. On the other hand, numerous segments of the society and the bulk of the population live in a state of undernourishment bordering on famine and an ever-growing crisis in housing. The social gap existing within each of these societies has reached a point where no solution can be envisaged. It is a vicious circle for, in the presence of such patterns of consumption, no solution can be found. It is, therefore, imperative that unless a radical change takes place on the political and social levels there is very little hope that these Arab societies can maintain a reasonable measure of stability. Somehow, it is ironic that these seemingly entrenched regimes may meet their unpleasant end as a result of their own impulsive inclinations against which they are powerless.

A further threat to their existence is their increasing reliance on a narrow ethnic, religious or social base of support. There has been a growing trend in Syria among the governing elite to depend entirely on the political support of the Alawites, a minority religious community. On the other hand, the greater majority of the Sunnis are being excluded from any significant share in power. In the recent elections for the Syrian parliament, the government had to extend for an extra day the deadline for voting, simply because less than 51 per cent of the eligible voters actually exercised their democratic right. This only goes to show how disinterested the adult Syrian population has become. In other Arab countries whenever a similar problem is faced, the government usually counts those who do not cast their votes as a positive vote for whoever is in power, thus living up to the well-known Arab proverb 'silence is the sign of agreement'.

To conclude, it is obvious that a Middle East settlement based on the assumption that certain key Arab regimes who are parties to it are going to last for some time to come, is indeed a very fragile settlement. It is probable that if and when some Syrian officer takes over power from Assad, he will not only condemn and abandon the commitment of his predecessor but may also justify his advent to power on the basis of championing the Palestinian cause. More important, he may claim that the 'corrupt regime' of his predecessor had betrayed the Arabs' most sacred cause, Palestine. As the political and economic situation stands today in some Arab countries, it is probable that a first communiqué may be heard one early morning declaring the collapse of all efforts towards peace in the region. If this is pessimism, then one ought to take a closer look at the Israeli position and see how great are the odds against a peaceful arrangement in the Middle East.

The general attitude of the Israelis is one of dragging their feet whenever a solution requiring territorial concessions is proposed. This attitude is expected to continue in any future negotiations. It may even be hardened as a result of some military and political changes which háve taken place in the area since October 1973. On the one hand, the hard-line attitude of the new Israeli government is in itself an obstacle to a major step towards a settlement. It would not be as easy as some may suggest for Menachem Begin to back down on some of the promises he made during the electoral campaign and to his followers since the establishment of the state of Israel in 1948. Indeed the measures his cabinet endorsed in the summer of 1977 concerning the establishment of a number of new Jewish settlements in the occupied territories only go to show how strongly entrenched is the feeling in Israel towards a policy of no concessions, even at the cost of the displeasure of the Americans. On the other hand, it is expected that the USA will use economic and military aid to Israel as a lever to counteract Israeli insurgency. But the magnitude of American influence on Israel has been highly exaggerated by the Arab regimes. The facts of the situation are probably different. In the long run while Israel largely depends on USA aid for survival, she has, however, since 1973, managed to gain a sizeable margin of economic and military independence. For example, it has been suggested that the Israeli economy can, under the present conditions, withstand American pressure for as long as some eighteen months. Militarily, the balance sheet has drastically changed in favour of Israel. Her ability to sustain an armed confrontation with the Arabs has increased. With the existing stock of arms, which Israel acquired from the USA, she may be able to enter a military conflict with the Arabs without resorting to the Americans except after months of fighting. This would allow Israel enough time to accomplish some more of her impressive feats in the Middle East. It is extremely difficult to ascertain whether any one of the front-line Arab regimes can or is prepared to cope with such a situation; most likely not.

Undoubtedly, since 1973, Israel has acquired a margin of military independence, and in a short-lived conflict, American pressure may have very little significance on the course of action Israel decides to take. In addition to this, the Arab regimes seem to forget that the American policy-maker frequently operates under the pressure of domestic restraints. One important restraint which he always faces, whenever the Middle East conflict is under consideration, is the pro-Israeli lobby in the Congress and the White House. Israel's position is not as vulnerable to American influence as it may have been during and some time after the October war. At that time, Israel was in desperate need of American assistance to survive the set-back she had sustained during the war. Today, the situation is different; the least one can say is that Israel is less amenable to American pressure than two years ago. Under such conditions, it is very difficult to imagine why Israel would be interested in a Middle East settlement. What possible gain is there to be achieved from a negotiated agreement with the Arabs? Israel's proposals submitted to Carter during Begin's recent visit to the USA do reflect a hard-headed mood on the part of the new administration in Israel. Of course, for the right price, such as billions of dollars from the USA, Arab recognition of Israel and the normalisation of political and economic relations with its Arab neighbours, Israel may consider pulling out from sizeable portions of Sinai and the Golan Heights. But as far as a new Palestinian state is concerned or a recognition of the PLO, the Israeli position is absolutely negative. One cannot help agreeing with the joint opinion of *The Times* correspondents in Cairo and Jerusalem that

> No matter how exaggerated are Arab expectations of Carter's influence on Israel, these nations [the Arabs] sincerely believe that the only road to peace leads through the White House. The danger for Carter is that if he fails to produce peace, he will be blamed vehemently by the Arabs and the region will be set perilously adrift, possibly toward war. In a bewildered bellicose mood, Israel quite conceivably could defy Carter's considerable leverage on that small country by opting for war.[3]

The prospect of Carter's failure will not stem from his inability to persuade Israel to surrender parts of the Syrian and Egyptian occupied territories, but from Israel's defiance in refusing to accept any arrangement which may involve accommodating the Palestinians. The Arab regimes recognise that in the long run any hope for a permanent peace and stability in the Middle East will require a solution to the Palestinian problem.

Finally, looking at the various elements which combine to render the current peace efforts less successful, one should consider the position of the Soviet Union. Undoubtedly the Russians, since 1972, have suffered a series of political set-backs in the region, which have undermined much of the influence they had acquired prior to that date. It has been such a frustrating experience for them to see their position gradually eroding in an area where they have made large financial and military investments. However, it would be wrong to imagine that their role has no bearing on the situation. The Russians still enjoy the friendship of Libya, Iraq and the PLO. It is true that their allies, at the moment, play a marginal role in setting the pace for the development of political events in the Middle East, but one cannot ignore the fact that they could add to the state of instability which exists in some of the front-line Arab countries. A case in point is the recent armed clashes between Libya and Egypt, and the persistent efforts of the regime in Iraq to undermine the position of Assad.

Considering the pros and cons of the current initiative for peace in the Middle East, it is possible to say that, while the short-term conditions are sufficiently adequate for a move towards peace, in the long run the more permanent elements for a durable peace seem to be lacking. These elements include Arab political and economic stability, Israeli moderation, Palestinian satisfaction and super-power consensus. There is little evidence to show that any of these factors are in the process of materialising in the near future. Does this mean that the alternative to a durable peace is war, as some observers have already concluded?[4]

One may differ with many observers' predictions concerning the prospect which may evolve if the present initiative for peace fails. If no progress towards a settlement is reached in the near future the probable consequence would be one of no peace—no war, a freezing of the situation. A prospect of this kind might prove to be very frustrating for some Arab regimes who have pinned all their hopes on 1977 to yield some solution, but disappointed or not they are in no position, with or

without aid, to do much about it. Life may become extremely difficult
for the front-line regimes, but still with financial support from the Arab
oil countries they may manage to make ends meet. Three significant
factors appear to contribute to their continued survival, despite their
political and economic bankruptcy. Firstly, these regimes have developed
a tight and relatively efficient system of internal security which has
been able to weaken the development of strong political opposition.
Secondly, due to the lack of organisation and determination on the part
of the opposition forces, the dissatisfied masses in these Arab societies
have no way of changing the political conditions. A mood of indifference and resignation seems to dominate their attitude towards the
national issues. Acting under pressure from economic difficulties they
have shown an unusual flexibility in adapting themselves to less expen-
sive and less nourishing diets. And on rare occasions when they become
restless and even violent, their actions have no political focus. In the
last few years, so many of the disturbances and riots which have taken
place in Egypt and Syria have simply petered out without any significant political consequences. Thirdly, the Arab front-line regimes have
constantly compensated for the lack of internal stability by aligning
themselves with one another and drawing on the support of one of the
super-powers.

However, to think that the Arab regimes would go to war if their
hopes in an American-sponsored peace settlement are frustrated would
be difficult to believe. Leaving aside the balance of military power in
the area which undoubtedly favours the Israelis, it is one thing for
these regimes to lead a fragile existence, but to risk war with Israel is
another. A possible alternative to the breakdown of the peace efforts
may not be war, but more likely a situation of no peace—no war. The
Arab regimes cannot afford a war nor is Israel being provoked into
launching one.

Under different conditions, war may become a probability. If, for
example, the chain of Arab solidarity breaks down as a result of a
political change in Egypt or Syria, a confrontation with Israel may
occur. The army in these two countries is the most likely candidate
for wresting power. A new military regime in either of these countries
would have to focus its attention on three vital issues, the economic
situation, the national question (occupied territories) and the Palestinian

cause. This does not mean that the new regime would be able to solve these problems. In fact the Arab experience with military regimes has been most disappointing. Still an army officer coming to power would have to appeal to his people by promising to remedy their most urgent problems for which the previous regime would normally be blamed. Needless to say, the economic problem would have top priority. The new regime would be faced with one of two alternatives, either to stretch its hand to the rich Arab countries or introduce measures which guarantee a more equitable distribution of wealth. Which of the two courses the new regime would take depends largely on the social nature of the new ruling elite and to some extent on the kind of attitude the conservative Arab oil countries take towards it. To opt for the first alternative would put the new regime in the same difficult position which led to the collapse of the earlier one. What would make more sense is for the new ruling elite to take radical measures internally to alleviate the plight of the masses. This would automatically put it at odds with the powerful rich Saudis and others. In terms of its Arab alliances, the new regime may find itself in a position where it has to depend on the Iraqi and Libyan regimes. Eventually, it may draw closer to the Soviet Union for financial and military support. The total effect of such changes, a radical social and economic policy internally and an alliance with the radical Arab regimes who take a less compromising attitude towards Israel, may result in a heightened state of tension between the new regime and Israel and the situation may eventually deteriorate into an armed confrontation. In the meantime, the PRM, especially if the change took place in Syria, would be encouraged to regain the positions it has lost in Lebanon and would once more gather momentum to act as an irritant to Israel. The American policy-maker may at this point become less interested in playing a peace-keeping mission in the Middle East. Instead the USA may move to curb the growing mood of insurgency among the Arabs and allow Israel to cut down to size the new radical Arab leadership in the region. In many respects a prospect of this kind would be almost a replay of the 1967 episode, but hopefully not with the same damaging effects for the Arabs.

Another prospect, a remote one, in which war would be on the agenda is if the new regime in one of the front-line countries falls not to the army but to political groups from the extreme right or the radical left.

Since 1967, there has been a growing tendency, in Egypt and countries of the Arab East, towards a break with the existing political and social values of society resulting from the continuous disappointments experienced by the Arab masses on all levels. This tendency has crystallised in two diametrically opposed political movements; one which seeks a break with the present, a return to what it identifies as the glorious past, and the other which draws its ideological inspiration from Marxism and preaches revolutionary change. Both movements reject the existing norms of society and aspire to make a fresh start. The former appeals to a wide segment of Arab and more specifically Egyptian society. It has gained some influence among the lower classes, especially those with a traditional education and a peasant background. The latter's support comes from a minority of middle-class intellectuals with a Western education and some segments of the working classes. Though the political significance of these movements cannot be gauged, it is, however, interesting to indicate that from the point of view of the governments involved they seem to pose a serious threat to the fabric of society. Since the beginning of 1977, the Egyptian government has moved on two occasions to suppress the members of the two movements. In January, following the food riots in Cairo, the government took the opportunity to clamp down on the left. Early in July, after the assassination of an ex-minister in Cairo, the government moved swiftly to suppress the extremist Islamic groups. In his speech commemorating the 25th anniversary of the Egyptian revolution Sadat significantly declared that his regime would not tolerate Marxist terrorism or Islamic fanaticism.

One should not exaggerate, as governments frequently do in the Middle East, the strength of such movements, but what would be useful is to understand the phenomenon. 'Extremism' in the Arab world seems to be the expression of utter disillusionment over the years with all the attempts made to establish viable political, social and economic arrangements. One generation of Arabs after another has passed through many kinds of different experiments aimed at reorganising society, but most of these experiments have proved to be futile and most disappointing. In their modern history, the Arabs have experienced or tried many forms of government: colonial rule, parliamentary democracy, monarchy, republic, socialism, military rule, etc. . . . No wonder, therefore, that tendencies which aim at breaking away from the existing conditions appear to gain some popularity and a fertile soil in the Arab world. When all hopes have been frustrated and the glaring old problems remain, then for the Arab peoples in the face of oppression, poverty and Israel, the only way of salvation would seem to be either God or revolution. If one day all the values that are cherished by the established orders are shattered and the reactionary conservatives or the revolutionaries come to power with a rejection of the traditional concepts of state, boundaries, diplomacy and the like, then the whole situation in the region may be open to a process of restructuring. The old may not disappear altogether, but the upsurge may set the Middle East on a course of development entirely different from what has been witnessed until today. In such a situation the Palestinian cause may reappear free of Arab restraints and the struggle against Israel would be renewed in the form of a holy war or a protracted people's war. It would not matter then whether Israel occupied an Arab town or even an Arab capital, what would be more important for those involved would be to pursue the fight with a Messianic conviction. It is perhaps relevant here to recall an earlier quotation from Gadhafi's message to Sadat, when the latter accepted the cease-fire in 1973: 'It would have been more honourable for us if we had continued the fight . . . The land may fall and buildings may collapse, but honour remains.'

When the leader of a fanatic group in Cairo was recently arrested, he expressed a similar mood of desperation and rejection. Outlining the aims of his society he claimed that society has been utterly corrupted, and he could see no hope of salvation for the pious few except by opting out of society and living in the deserts and mountains. There they would pass into a period of religious meditation and spiritual purification after which they would descend on society, conquer it and establish God's kingdom on earth. The idea is not new; the history of Islam is full of such attempts. The Wahhabi movement started and still maintains some of these notions, but what is surprising in present-day Arab society is to have a relatively large number of adherents involved in such a movement. Despite the vigilance of the internal security machine in Egypt, the leader of the new group could claim a membership in his organisation amounting to 4,000 men and women. The significance of such a figure, even if it is slightly exaggerated cannot be underestimated. It would seem that what often appears to the sophisticated mind to be simple and naïve, even utopian, may under certain conditions gain a wide appeal among frustrated, desperate men. Once this happens these ideas may become real forces and society has to recognise them.

One can imagine a similar scenario outlined by the Arab left, but the ideological expression would certainly differ. The rearrangement of society and the struggle for its emancipation from the stifling restraints of the present may be understood differently, but in the final analysis a change from the grass-roots is envisaged: a change which would radically disrupt the social and political fabric and dismantle the system of values upheld by the ruling classes and in favour of a more populist structure of society and an outlook which totally rejects the existing social and political conditions.

To sum up, it is relatively difficult to make any predictions concerning the political development of the situation in the Middle East. It would seem that the most one can do is to pick up some of the more significant indications that we have today and try to analyse them in the light of the possible directions Arab society may take. In the process, one should bear in mind that once speculation is allowed to intervene, the gauging of variables becomes much more difficult. At present, what we have is an initiative towards a settlement of the Middle East conflict; the likelihood of an agreement seems to be there, an agreement sponsored by the Americans. However, the odds against it are tremendous. Some may think that it is not even worth the effort. Most of the speculation that has been going on for some time is centering around it. However, though the current discussion makes a very interesting exercise in the interaction of international and regional politics, yet the main drawback to the implementation of a plan or plans of action agreed upon by the parties concerned, lies in the lack of the appropriate conditions for a permanent solution. A plan may very well evolve in Geneva after a series of tedious negotiations, but the conditions for a durable peace in the Middle East require the political and social long-term stability of the Arab regimes and demand a large measure of Israeli flexibility. Neither of these two conditions is in existence in the Middle East situation today, and therefore, other scenarios become more relevant. At best a scenario of no peace—no war may continue, but at worst drastic changes may take place in some Arab societies and consequently lead to a state of permanent conflict among Arabs and between some Arabs and Israel.

August 1977

Notes

1. Further references to the Arab regimes, unless specified will mean the coalition of Arab countries mentioned above.
2. *The Times*, 3 August 1977.
3. *The Times*, 25 July 1977.
4. Anthony Nutting, *Spectator*, 6 August 1977, pp. 16-19.

4 SADAT'S PEACE INITIATIVE AND THE PALESTINIAN QUESTION

Sadat's visit to Jerusalem in November 1977 was not the outcome of a divine revelation nor the result of a sudden realisation on his part and that of Begin that wars lead to the loss of human life and the misery of an increasing number of orphans and widows. In retrospect it would seem that Sadat's peace initiative was the natural product of a policy which some Arab regimes had adopted even before Sadat came to power in late 1970. It might be traced back to the time when Egypt accepted the UN Resolution 242, soon after the 1967 June war. In 1970, Nasser was more inclined to endorse a peaceful settlement based on Rogers' ill-fated plan. Though such a policy was interrupted for a short interval by the October War of 1973, yet by and large, the efforts and hopes of the Arab regimes continued to focus on a peaceful agreement.

It would seem that in the years following the Arab defeat in 1967, the Arab stand was largely determined by the lack of military preparedness and economic instability of the front-line Arab states. In time, the Arab regimes, notably Egypt, appeared to be more intent than ever in the history of the Arab-Israeli conflict to reach a peaceful settlement. Setting aside the misleading claim made by the Egyptian leadership that it was negotiating from a position of strength, it was quite clear that since the early 1970s, Egypt had embarked on new internal and external policies.

The new disposition ought to be considered in relation to the evolution of a new ruling class under Sadat with its special vested interests, privileges and ambitions. The policies of Sadat were closely linked to such a change in the political and social fabric of Egyptian society.

Up to the early 1960s, most of the literature concerned with analysing the Nasserite era centered around the role of the army officers in Egyptian politics. By the mid 1960s, however, there appeared a growing awareness of the fact that in time, the military merged with other professional and social groups largely drawn from the middle classes to form the ruling elite of Egypt. It was noticed that with the drastic socialist measures taken in 1961, an increasing number of technocrats, experts, bureaucrats, members of the liberal professions and the labour aristocracy was incorporated in the higher echelons of the state administration. At their disposal were the state apparatus and the public sector through which they controlled the economic life of the country.

Under Sadat and the three-year-old economic 'open door' policy, the position of the different groups within the ruling class had been consolidated. Their interests became much more closely interlinked and their social and economic relations more cohesive. Soon after the 1967 defeat and the weakening of the public sector, they took control of the private sector and sought to promote their interests through it by freeing it from the previous restraints imposed by Nasser. The bulk of the ruling elite came to be represented by the ex-army officer turned politician, the contractor who made huge profits out of the government construction projects, the landowner who benefited from the loopholes in the successive land reform laws, the local agent of the Japanese, European and American interests, and last but not least, the old *pasha* who took advantage of the liberalising policies of the regime. Together these elements formed the upper class of Egyptian society; they possessed the wealth as well as the power and exercised political and economic hegemony over the rest of the population.

The new changes in the structure of society and power led to a number of major consequences. Perhaps most important among them was Egypt's growing reliance on the United States instead of her old ally the Soviet Union. From 1967 to 1971, two competing parties appeared within the ranks of the Egyptian ruling elite. One opted for the maintenance of political power in the hands of those in control of such state organisations as the Arab Socialist Union, the public sector and the police; the other sought to vest all powers in the newly emerging upper class. In May 1971, the conflict between the two factions was resolved in favour of the latter group. From then onward, the regime had been well disposed towards a system of government which would transfer gradually the powers of the state apparatus built under Nasser to the hands of the upper segments in society. Thus, political parties were established, restrictions on export-import trade and investment of foreign capital were lifted, and moves towards the dismantling of the public sector were taken. This was necessarily accompanied by the crucial step of replacing Egypt's alliance with the Soviet Union by one with the USA.

The Soviet influence in Egypt traditionally tended to strengthen the grip of the state bourgeoisie. It also prevented the upper classes outside the state apparatus from benefiting from the economic relations between Egypt and the Eastern Bloc. However, with the advent of Sadat to power, the doors were thrown wide open for the export-import merchant, the contractor and the land speculator, not to mention the foreign investor, to play the major role in the economic life of Egypt. Such a development in the situation did not only undermine the position of the public sector and the social classes dependent on it, but also alienated the Soviet leadership.

Though the Soviet Union soon after Sadat's take-over in May 1971, attempted to save the situation by signing a treaty of friendship with Egypt, yet a year later the anti-Soviet campaign was in full swing and eventually the treaty was abrogated by Sadat. Some of the early criticisms against the Soviet Union focused around the issue of arms supplies to Egypt. After the withdrawal of the Soviet technicians and military mission from Egypt in July 1972, Sadat did not lose much time in accusing the Soviet leadership of dragging its feet on arms deliveries. Furthermore, the government-controlled press and mass media conveyed the strong impression that Soviet military equipment was generally inferior to anything the Americans handed to Israel. Though Sadat paid some lip-service to the Russian stand during the October war in 1973, he continued shortly afterwards, however, to express his bitter enmity towards the former ally of Egypt.

The anti-Soviet position of Sadat's regime extended to the internal political forces in Egypt who advocated radical solutions for the problems of their society. Marxists and Nasserites were labelled by Sadat as agents of the Soviet Union, and the internal security machine was kept on the alert harassing them and maintaining a close watch over their activities. In late 1976, when the transport workers' strike disrupted public communications in Cairo, the Prime Minister immediately blamed some eleven trade unionists, whom he described as 'communists', for the strike. Similarly, during the food riots of January 1977, the Ministry of the Interior without hesitation or any investigation found no scapegoat for its own shortcomings for keeping order in the country except those it referred to as 'communist agitators'. Security efforts following the riots revealed that in all of Egypt there were not more than 200 activists with radical leanings distributed among four secret organisations. Such a fact could not account by any stretch of the imagination for the widespread and largescale events which took place during the riots. The overreaction of the regime against the radical forces went as far as to stifle their voices in the press. By mid-1977, the publications of the 'nationalised left' in Egypt were silenced. The monthly *al-Tali'a* disappeared and the chief editor of the two left-wing weeklies *Rosa el-Youssef* and *Sabah el Khair* resigned his post. The new ruling class of Egypt appeared to be over-sensitive to anything that had to do with the Soviet Union, communism or even Nasserism. On the other hand a more welcoming attitude was extended to the USA and her regional allies Iran and Saudi Arabia. To all intents and purposes, Egypt, despite all the risks involved, chose to forego her close relations with the Soviet Union, and moved to rely completely on the USA. In the long run such a step might prove to be extremely harmful to Egypt's economic and military capabilities, but then why should one assume that any of the ruling classes in the Arab world were at all interested in the future of their societies?

The Arab regimes with very few exceptions are mainly concerned with the preservation of power. The upper classes in Arab societies who back the men in power and at the same time utilise them to enhance their own economic interests are equally short-sighted. They do not represent anything similar to the Western bourgeois classes. In the West, the bourgeoisie grew out of the collapse of the feudal system and built a new society by launching 'the commercial and industrial revolutions'. In the course of its development, the Western bourgeoisie came to dominate other societies in Africa, Asia and Latin America. The upper class in the Arab world, conveniently called the Arab bourgeoisie, was at best an agent class. It played the role of the middle man between the interests of the foreigners and its own society. By virtue of its subordination for a long time to the changes occurring outside its borders and being entirely dependent on the fluctuations of the international capitalist market, the local bourgeoisie operated on the basis of short-term opportunities. In the final analysis, it was never in a position to determine its own future let alone that of its society. Most of the time, it was on the alert waiting for an opportunity to seize. In time, the so-called bourgeois class emerged in the Arab world with a psychological disposition which was cautious, hesitant, short-sighted and lacking a sense of community or social obligation towards the rest of society. It had no long-term plans for the economic development of society and was interested only in power to perpetuate its exploitation of the lower classes.

The attitude of the Arab bourgeoisie towards political power rendered its maintenance of that power rather shaky and at best short-lived. Unaware of the requirements of political legitimacy, it often resorted to force in order to achieve its ends. Ultimately, it turned out to be a self-defeating social class, with a built-in inability to see the long-term interests of the society as a whole, which is a necessary condition for political stability. The misfortune of the Arab bourgeoisie stemmed from the fact that it had been brought to life at an inopportune moment in history, a moment largely characterised by the hegemony of Western capitalism. It played and continued to play the role of a parasitic class without any productive function. It fed on the efforts of the mass of working Arabs, and appropriated the surplus they produced in the course of serving its Western masters.

The new upper classes of Egypt, which appeared after 1967 had similar, even identical, features to the Egyptian bourgeoisie which existed before 1952, but the difference between them was one of social origins. Before 1952, the bourgeoisie owed its origin to an alliance of the local capitalists and segments of the large land-owning class; the new bourgeoisie had been the product of some sections of the middle classes which came to power in the post-1952 period. More recently, they were joined by the remnants of the old *pasha* class. The dependence of Sadat's regime on the support of such social classes rendered its efforts to solve the problems of the masses futile.

Firstly, in spite of the fact that Egypt had received great amounts of aid since 1973, yet the new bourgeoisie managed to squander a large portion of it on unproductive projects which only benefited the well-to-do classes. The growing polarisation of wealth and power, in the absence of a social class taking upon itself the task of economic development, left the bulk of the population in a state of existence worse than ever before. Secondly, for three decades Egypt had been involved in one war after another, thus depleting her resources. She had lost men, money and territory, and still nothing in the recent political developments in the region had indicated an end to this state of affairs in the near future. As long as she maintained her relations with the Soviet Union, Egypt succeeded in reaching a reasonable level of military preparedness without incurring too much of the costs. However, once she opted for American friendship she appeared to trade off military preparedness for a political settlement. Unfortunately, she lost both. Though the American administration seemed to be willing to provide Egypt with some warplanes, yet it was in no way prepared to establish anything near military parity between Egypt and Israel. 'The Israelis already have clear air superiority', a senior USA official insisted when commenting on the sale of the American warplanes to Egypt, and 'if it's been eroded, it's been from 10-to-1 to 9-to-1'.[1]

In the light of this, one wonders what was the real reason behind Sadat's anti-Soviet attitude. If he was dissatisfied with the Soviet insensitivity to his military needs, as he repeatedly pointed out, then the USA did not make a better offer. Similarly, if he had hoped that the USA would present him with a satisfactory political settlement, no such act had yet materialised. The remaining explanation might be sought in the fact that the West had provided the new bourgeoisie of Egypt with better and more lucrative opportunities than the Soviet Union. Signs of luxury consumption by the few had become a major characteristic of Cairo next to mass poverty. The society columns in the Egyptian weeklies reappeared and the names of the old and new celebrities were preceded by such descriptions as the millionaire, the financial magnate and the *pasha*.

The main priority of the Nasserite regime was to establish middle-class socialism. This objective determined the kind of allies Egypt chose on the Arab and international levels. Consequently, it provoked the enmity of the conservative Arab regimes, the West and Israel. Under these circumstances, a state of tension was perpetuated in the region. On the other hand, Sadat's objectives were geared to satisfying the newly emerging bourgeoisie. The situation, therefore, required closer relations with the West, cordiality with the conservative Arabs and an understanding with Israel. The less tension the area experienced, the more benefits were enjoyed by the compradors of Egypt. What the future held for them was none of their concern; they were neither interested nor prepared to give it much thought. If history had a lesson to teach, they chose to mystify it. The downfall of the old bourgeoisie in 1952 was seen as a dark spot in the history of Egypt. It legitimised any banal attack against Nasserism and consequently allowed for its elimination from the recent history of Egypt. Thus a convenient way was discovered over the dead body of Nasserism. It bridged the gap between the old bourgeoisie and the new one, without holding either of them responsible for the miseries of the past or the present.

A further consequence of the rise of the new bourgeoisie to power necessitated a shift in Egypt's position towards the PRM and the Palestinian people. Since the early 1920s, the Arab regimes had exploited the Palestinian question in the course of inter-Arab rivalry and in their efforts to play one foreign power against another. However, it was also true that some of the Arab ruling classes, including the Egyptian, viewed the creation of the state of Israel in 1948 as a threat to their own ambitions. In other words, the involvement of some Arab countries in the struggle against Zionism and Israel was a result of a genuine clash of interests between them and the newly established entity in their midst. In the case of Egypt, it became increasingly clear that its participation in the first Arab-Israeli war in 1948 was due to a number of factors. One of them was King Farouk's keen desire to gain for himself the position of leadership in the Arab world *vis-à-vis* serious contenders, especially King Abdullah of Jordan. At the same time, public opinion in Egypt seemed to favour such an involvement. Before Egypt had formally entered the war, the Muslim Brethren were already dispatching their trained volunteers to the front. But perhaps the most important factor was the attitude of Egypt's ruling class towards the emergence of an alien political entity separating it from the Arab East.

After the Second World War, the Egyptian bourgeoisie had hoped to expand its activities to the Arab countries east of Sinai. The Bank Misr Group which included among its members the leading entrepreneurs of Egypt had since its establishment in 1920 made one attempt after another to penetrate the Arab markets. Most of its efforts were thwarted by the economic measures taken by the occupying powers, France and England. It was not until the end of the Second World War that

many of the Arab countries gained their independence and Bank Misr was given an equal opportunity to compete with foreign interests. Following the withdrawal of the French from Syria and Lebanon, the Bank established branches in the capitals of the two countries.
Trade with the countries of the Arab East experienced a boom and was facilitated by the railway network which linked Egypt to the Arab East via Palestine.

The creation of Israel did not only form a geographical obstacle to Egypt's access to its natural markets in the East, but the new state also posed a serious threat to the growing interests of the Egyptian bourgoisie in the region. By virtue of its close links with the West and the world-wide reputation that Jewish communities enjoyed as a hard-working and business-minded people, Israel appeared to be more quali-fied than any other country in the region for a dominant economic role. This thought caused great concern among the Egyptian entre-preneurs as they realized that little room would be left for them if Jewish capital and effort used Israel as an economic base to penetrate the Arab region. Egyptian products, technical know-how and contacts with the business community in the West were considered to be no match for those of Israel. Israeli industrial products of a quality similar to that of the best in the West would have eventually squeezed out those of Egypt from the Middle Eastern markets. Therefore, it was thought necessary for Egypt in 1948 to prevent the emergence of the state of Israel. However, when this failed, Egypt led the Arabs in an economic embargo against Israel which has lasted until today.

After 1952 and the rise of Nasser to power, the new ruling class, which controlled the public sector and formed a state bourgeoisie, con-tinued to view Israel as an obstacle to its political and economic ambi-tions in the Arab East. The reality of the Israeli threat became much more obvious during the Suez War in 1956. This was reinforced by Israel's persistence in tying any proposal for peace in the Middle East with a demand for the normalisation of economic relations with the Arab countries.

Under Sadat, the stand of the ruling class towards Israel has under-gone a change, especially since 1973. When Sadat first showed signs of moving towards a peaceful settlement, he asserted that while an agree-ment on ending the state of war and recognising Israel could be achieved in no time, he thought, however, that peace in the sense of normalising relations on all levels was not feasible and required another generation of Arabs and Israelis to work it out. By mid-1977, he predicted that an over-all solution to the conflict needed some five years before it could be achieved. But on his recent visit to the USA in early 1978, he claimed that peace could be achieved in a matter of weeks if not days.

It appeared that the new bourgeoisie of Egypt had gradually adopted a new view of the conflict. Despite the fact that in an agreement with Egypt, Israel would still seek to open 'new commercial markets for exports',[2] the Egyptian ruling class seemed to be less sensitive to the issue than before. Sadat's journey to Jerusalem might be regarded as a sincere effort on his part to achieve peace. It might also be viewed as a major political move to strengthen his hand in future negotiations with the Israelis. Furthermore, the trip to Jerusalem had won Sadat the support of public opinion in the West and many parts of the Arab world, especially among the well-to-do segments of Arab society. Most important, he had been able to win his own people. However, most of the gains made were temporary and would account only in a marginal way for the steps he had taken towards peace. Sadat could not hope to sustain the support of public opinion even at home for ever. For this he needed a propaganda machine in the West similar to that of the Zionist movement to preserve his gains. Soon after the trip, changes were detected in Israel where 'Public opinion tends to the extreme and fluctuates wildly. Thus 90% of the Israelis thought during Sadat's November visit that peace with Egypt was possible; now 60% believe there will be another war within ten years.'[3] Even in Egypt the euphoria which accompanied the visit had gradually subsided.

More important than the temporary gains made by Sadat's peace initiative was the fact that his visit to Israel was a reflection of a determined desire on the part of the Egyptian regime and the new bourgeoisie to reach a compromise with the West and Israel. The Egyptian bourgeoisie did not seem to be too concerned with a potential Israeli threat to dominate the region economically. Some of the Egyptian entrepreneurs, the parasites of the new economic 'open door' policy, had convinced themselves of the idea that the time was ripe for launching joint economic ventures with Israeli and foreign businessmen. King Hassan of Morocco in the course of supporting Sadat's initiative expressed such a mood. He predicted future miracles, once Arab capital and Jewish genius joined hands. Unlike the old bourgeoisie, the new Egyptian bourgeoisie did not envisage a potential clash of interest between it and an Israel bent for the first time since her creation on opening new markets for her commercial exports. One reason for this seemingly careless attitude was perhaps due to the immaturity of the newly emerging bourgeoisie in Egypt. After all, it was only a decade or so old and, with the exception of a small section of it, it was still feeling its way through the intricate relationships of the international and local markets.

More recently, the Egyptian bourgeoisie had come to the conclusion, perhaps with some encouragement from the USA that great tasks were awaiting it in Africa. Sadat's emphasis on his responsibilities in Africa had increasingly been more frequent. On returning from his first visit to the USA in 1977 he dispatched some of his Air Force technicians and combat units to assist the Zaire government repelling the Angolan revolutionaries. Again, once the Somali-Ethiopian conflict erupted in Ogaden he did not refrain from pledging his full political and military support to Somalia. And as the conflict between Chad and Libya threatened to break out, he immediately took a stand on the side of Chad. Furthermore, as Egypt's relations with some countries of the Arab East deteriorated, Sadat turned his attention towards the south. The Egyptian regime thus revived the old concept of the unity of the Nile Valley and hardly a day passed without the exchange of visits between the officials of the two countries at the highest level. By early 1978, Egypt was distinctly bent on playing a major role in African affairs while its role east of Sinai seemed to decline. Even the call for an Arab summit made by Saudi Arabia and the Gulf countries was welcomed only half-heartedly in Egypt.

The ruling class of Egypt had led itself to believe that the new American strategy in the region had assigned Egypt a central role in Africa; a role which did not require Egypt to be a party to the Arab-Israeli conflict, because the USA had accurately defined the division of labour in the region. In this respect, Israel, Iran and Saudi Arabia were responsible for keeping order in the Arab East and safeguarding American interests. Their main function was to prevent any of the Arab regimes or a coalition of political and military forces in the area from becoming so powerful as to disturb the flow of oil to the West.

On the other hand, Egypt together with the other pro-American regimes in Africa were entrusted with the task of containing the spread of communism in black Africa and acting as an economic base for Western commercial exports. The outstanding problem which remained to be solved was for the USA to search for a satisfactory solution to the Egyptian-Israeli conflict. Once an accommodation was reached, the Egyptian bourgeoisie would then promote its own interests at the expense of its African neighbours under the most conducive conditions, brought about by peace, stability and the flow of foreign capital into Cairo. By the same token, Israel would be able, once Egypt was neutralised, to subdue her intransigent neighbours and once and for all keep them in check. A case in point was the attack launched by Israel against southern Lebanon in March 1978. With Egypt practically neutralised, and the PRM unable to defend its bases, the Syrian army in Lebanon watched impotently the conquest of the south.

Whether the USA had drawn up such a strategy or not was beside the point, so long as the ruling class of Egypt believed in it and acted accordingly. As a matter of fact, all the evidence went to show that Sadat was more than willing to play the part allotted to him in that strategy. The recent involvement of Egypt in Africa has been consistent with the American stand in that part of the world.

A major requirement of Egypt's new role following Sadat's visit to Jerusalem, was to dissociate itself as much as possible from the Palestinian question; better still, to dissociate itself from the Arab East. Since the Arab defeat in 1967, and despite the relative military success of Syria and Egypt in October 1973, a mood of anti-Arab feeling had been noticeable among the majority of Egyptian officials and intellectuals, with a few exceptions, and wide segments of public opinion. The Arabs were held responsible for Egypt's problems. Observers often heard intelligent Egyptians arguing that had Egypt kept out of the Arabs' wars with Israel, had she not been involved with the Syrians in schemes of Arab unity, and had she not ventured into supporting a republican regime in Yemen in 1962, she would have fared much better on her own. Regularly it was claimed that the price of Egypt's commitments to the Arab problems had depleted her resources and brought about all kinds of political, economic and military disasters. On the official level some lip-service to Arabism had been paid but only in the course of describing how much Egypt had sacrificed for the Arab cause. On the whole, however, the government-controlled propaganda machine had encouraged and nurtured the hostile tendency, or at least did not bother to dispel some of the flagrant inaccuracies and exaggerations. At no time did the government attempt to enlighten its own public opinion of the real reasons concerning Egypt's involvement in the politics of the Arab region.

The campaign against Arabism in Egypt focused more on the Palestinian issue than any other problem due to its apparent central position in the concerns of the governments and peoples of the Arab world. In a similar fashion to communism, but to a greater degree, Palestine became the scapegoat for most of the problems encountered by the Arab ruling classes. In the name of Palestine some of the worst crimes against the rights of the Arab people were committed. And in the name of Palestine some of the worst problems of Arab society caused by the Arab ruling classes were excused. The Arab peoples were always reminded that their right for a democratic life was not possible without first liberating the occupied territories. At the same time they were told that whatever misery they suffered from was necessary for the sake of achieving for the Palestinians the right of self-determination.

An image of the Palestinian cause had been painted which left the Arab peoples, except the well-informed among them, with very little sympathy for the plight of the Palestinian Arabs. Eventually, the time came for Egypt, especially following Sadat's peace initiative to effect a break with the Palestinian question. In other front-line countries, the break had occurred earlier, in Jordan in 1970, in Syria and Lebanon in 1976.

Following the June war in 1967, the Arab regimes tended to exaggerate beyond any proportion the growing influence of the PRM. Government officials, journalists and intellectuals praised the Palestinians for continuing the fight when the Arab enemies laid down their arms in surrender or defeat. The Palestinian 'freedom fighter', 'commando', *'fida'i'*, 'man of the resistance', etc. . . became the idol of the Arab masses and the symbol of Arab defiance. Gradually, however, the Arab regimes began to pose some questions as to the achievements of the new idol. How much of Palestine had he liberated? Who was financing him? Where was his proper place: in the Arab towns or facing the enemy on the front? The main purpose of these questions was to show that the PRM was neither in a position to liberate any part of the Palestinian territory nor seriously concerned with the problems of the Palestinian people.

King Hussein, soon after the Karameh battle in March 1968, when Fateh gained a lot of popularity, set to work to discredit the PRM. Towards the end of 1970, he succeeded in indoctrinating the rank and file of his army as well as his East Jordanian subjects to view the PLO as their worst and most hated enemy. Consequently, in September of the same year he was able with the full backing of his army to drive the PRM out of Jordan.

In October 1973, Syria and Egypt managed to steal the show from the PRM. During this war both countries performed relatively well in the battle-field and regained some of their lost credibility. From that time onwards, the idea of achieving a solution for the Palestinian question at the hands of the Arab governments began to acquire more momentum. The initiative once more shifted to the hands of the Arab ruling classes after it had been left in the hands of the PRM from 1967 to 1973. During the Lebanese Civil War, Syrian and Lebanese public opinion was gradually alienated. Every effort was made by the governments of the two countries to discredit the Palestinian resistance. In the final analysis, the Syrian army, which had been brought up since independence on the idea of regarding Palestine as the most sacred Arab cause, turned its guns against the armed vanguard of the Palestinian people. It was not only a matter of adhering to military discipline, but more than that it was a matter of years of anti-Palestinian propaganda within the ranks of the army fostered by the ruling Baath party. It was ironic to hear at the time of the civil war in Lebanon, the Syrian broad-casting station levelling against the PRM the same accusations made a few years earlier by Radio Amman. Suddenly Assad of Syria excused Hussein for massacring the Palestinian militants in September 1970. Finally, Egypt joined the ranks of the anti-Palestinian camp and took the opportunity of Sadat's visit to Israel to sever its links with the Palestinian cause.

The early differences between Egypt and the PLO occurred when Nasser accepted the Rogers Plan in July 1970. Immediately measures

were taken to close down the Voice of the Palestine Revolution trans-
mitting from Cairo, and Nasser announced that while he appreciated
the position of the PRM on the issue, he could not neglect his duties as
a statesman. The second major occasion on which the PLO and the
Egyptian regime clashed was when Sadat accepted the second Sinai
agreement. In that instance, accusations were exchanged between the
two sides, and once more the Voice of the Palestine Revolution was
closed down. Furthermore, measures were taken by the Egyptian
authorities to restrict the activities of the PLO representatives in Cairo.

However, the recent visit of Sadat to Israel brought about a severe
and perhaps a final break in Egyptian-Palestinian relations. The Egyptian ruling class with the new perception it had developed concerning
its role in the region rapidly moved into a position of dissociating itself
from the Palestinian issue. Unlike the Jordanian monarch who continued to maintain an interest in the Palestinian question, and especially
in the West Bank, the Egyptian leadership did not entertain any claim
to any part of Palestine. The break was not as sudden as it might
appear, but has evolved gradually during the last decade. After each
incident in which the two parties confronted each other, feelings hardened and suspicions, accusations and counter-accusations became
increasingly more vicious. Behind it all was this determined effort on
the part of the Egyptian ruling class encouraged by its American ally to
reach a compromise with Israel and once and for all turn Egypt's attention away from the problems of the Arab East to those of Africa.

The Egyptian regime proceeded to implement the new policy on a
number of levels. First, it was necessary to sway public opinion from a
position of enthusiastic involvement in the Palestinian cause nurtured
by the government for almost three decades to that of hostile dissociation. Among a population with a high illiteracy rate, the regime had
very little difficulty in changing the minds of the people. Apart from
blaming Palestine for whatever economic problems Egypt faced, the
government-controlled propaganda machine focused on two issues. It
condemned all acts of violence carried out by some of the Palestinian
fringe groups as terrorism directed against Sadat's efforts for peace, and
held on to the obsession of winning over public opinion in the West and
especially in the USA. The latter tendency went so far as to exclude
other means of achieving a satisfactory solution to the Arab-Israeli con-

flict.

Public opinion in Egypt and to some extent other Arab countries came to believe that the road to the establishment of a castrated Palestinian state in the West Bank and Gaza, and the regaining of the Arab territories lost in 1967, could only be secured by converting more people in the West to the Arab point of view. In fact other factors contributing to a settlement in the Middle East, such as military preparedness and the use of oil as a political leverage, were given up for diplomacy.

Eventually, the handling of the conflict with Israel in the Arab world and Egypt was left to a handful of politicians and in some cases, a single individual. Sadat took pride in the fact that before going on his trip to Jerusalem, he consulted only with his Foreign Minister. The latter disagreed with him and immediately resigned, but that did not prevent the President from going through with his plans. Sadat did not misjudge the reaction of his people. The grounds were already prepared for taking such a step without provoking any significant hostility. By the time, Sadat returned from his trip, the Egyptian street, almost to a man, was in support of his action. The country appeared as if it had resigned its right to decide on a major national issue to one man.

A more dangerous manipulation of the so-called Palestinian terrorism was employed in displacing the old enmity towards Israel with an equal, if not stronger, hostility towards the Palestinian people and Palestine. The assassination of Youssef el-Siba'i, chief editor of *al-Ahram* provoked strong feelings of hate against the Palestinians. The government was not disturbed by the change of attitude among the masses. On the contrary, at the funeral, the Prime Minister appeared rather pleased to hear the angry crowds next to him shouting 'No more Palestine after today'. Neither the local press nor the government sources of information bothered to clarify the position of the PLO, which condemned the assassination in no uncertain terms. Even when *al-Ahram* later decided to publish extracts from the PLO statement, it followed them up with a commentary which laid the responsibility for the assassination squarely on the PLO's head. Similarly, the ill-fated Egyptian commando attack on Larnaka to capture the assassins was presented to the Egyptian public as a heroic attempt which was betrayed by the President of Cyprus assisted by a Palestinian military unit sent by Arafat from Beirut.

It was most unfortunate that the victim of the Larnaka incident was el-Siba'i. His assassination played right into the hands of the Egyptian regime. No effort was lost to exploit the event to the full. El-Siba'i, a free officer, novelist and journalist who had accompanied Sadat on his trip to Israel had during the last thirty years or more produced so much literary work of varying quality and entered the homes of all classes of Egyptians. His novels were read by the young and the old, the rich and the poor; they were introduced to the illiterate public by the cinema and television. He had a very wide and sympathetic audience among the Egyptians. His assassination by two Palestinians, who obviously did not belong to any of the well-known or significant organisations, did not endear the cause of Palestine any more to the Egyptian people. 'No Palestine after today', sounded as if Egypt had finally turned its back on the Palestinian cause.

Furthermore, in the course of condemning terrorism, the Egyptian government condemned the PLO. Despite the fact that Sadat did not formally withdraw Egypt's recognition of the PLO, however, since his trip to Jerusalem, he had been searching for a substitute to it, a substitute which would bless his steps towards a peaceful settlement. In his speech to the Israeli Knesset, he did not refer at all to the PLO, and once in Cairo he often referred to the notables of the West Bank and Gaza as the real representatives of the Palestinian people. At the same time he described the leadership of the PLO as armchair militants who spent their time in night-clubs.

The Egyptian regime through the efficient use of the mass media and the deliberate exploitation of Palestinian adventurism had been able to discredit the legitimate leadership of the Palestinian Revolution and turn Egyptian public opinion dead against it. However, if the illiterate Egyptian public had been indoctrinated in stages to adopt such a position, how did the majority of Egyptian thinkers and intellectuals accept a similar stand?

Following Sadat's initiative, the better informed elements of Egyptian society praised the move without any reservations. Some hailed Sadat as the maker of peace and recorded an endless list of benefits which they imagined Egypt was about to enjoy. In time, however, more sober reactions surfaced. Some independent left-wing thinkers and a number of journalists and intellectuals concerned for Egypt's relations with the Arab world appeared to deal with the subject on 'more realistic grounds.' Surprisingly enough, their views tended to reinforce those which were repeated by the authorities. As a matter of fact, they expressed themselves in pretty much the same way as did the apologists for the regime and government officials. Their starting point was to claim that the initiative was based on a realistic reading of the international and regional political situations. Tawfiq al-Hakim, the well-known Egyptian writer, explained that this support for Sadat was based on the latter's 'logical and realistic thinking and attitude'.[4] He urged the political parties in Egypt to adopt neutrality as part of their political programmes. What he meant by Egyptian neutrality was not an independent stand from the Eastern and Western Blocs, but neutrality with respect to the Arabs. He wrote:

> The Arabs now have the money and the men. They have reached adulthood and do not need to burden Egypt with their problems and concerns . . . As for Egypt's army, it should be a defensive army, strong and equipped with modern weapons so as to protect its neutrality.[5]

In effect, al-Hakim was advocating Egypt's dissociation from the Arabs. Similarly, the playwright Yousif Idriss declared:

> I support Sadat's Egyptian, popular and peaceful initiative, a stand which may not be understood by our Arab brethren . . . We in Egypt do not have the means of rejection or war. Rejection requires a strong economy which would enable you to say 'no' without dying of hunger, or prostituting your women and daughters for a handful of bread.[6]

Other Egyptian intellectuals known for their radical leanings presented a more intersting view. Louis Awad, one-time university professor, journalist and outstanding thinker, in an article entitled 'A Left-Wing Vision Concerning the Peace Initiative' rationalised his endorsement of Sadat's move by using the argument of the impossible. He claimed that a radical solution to the Arab-Israeli conflict could only be achieved through armed struggle. He asserted, however, that such a course of action would have necessarily led to the Vietnamisation of the region. But in view of the fact that none of the Arab regimes, including Egypt, were ready to take a risk of that kind, then the only option open to them was to adopt peaceful means. Thus, the political solution was given priority over the military one.[7] In other words, since it was impossible, in Awad's opinion, for the region to take a revolutionary Vietnam-like solution, the Egyptian leadership, therefore, had no choice but to accept the other extreme, namely to go to Jerusalem, hat in hand, ready to recognise the state of Israel.

The question, however, remained unanswered. Did the absence of a revolutionary alternative legitimise a drift away from Arabism and justify Egypt's new stand? If the conditions for Vietnamisation were not available, then should the intellectuals rush to confer their blessings on the Arab regimes who stifled the growth of a revolutionary potential? For the Arab thinker the only alternative was certainly not to accept the defection of his government. Arab intellectuals instead of employing themselves with the task of rationalising the compromising actions of the Arab regimes might have done much better to launch an ideological struggle against the justification given in support of an attitude of oppression and surrender.

With the incorporation of a large segment of the Egyptian intelligentsia in the new drive for dissociating Egypt from the Arab problems and the Palestinian question, only one pocket of resistance remained, namely, the Party of Patriotic Coalition. In 1976, Sadat by a presidential decree allowed the formation of three political parties to represent an arbitrary division of political tendencies in Egypt. These included the left, known as the Patriotic Coalition, the right, and the ruling party, better known as the Party of Egypt. A fourth party was later organised, the New Wafd Party representing the old *pasha* class and a section of the new bourgeoisie. The left consisted of a broad alliance of forces which included the ex-communists, some Marxist intellectuals and a wide range of Nasserite and liberal elements. The left advocated among other things the unity of the Arabs in their struggle against the USA and Israel. Its ideological commitment to the Palestine cause and the PLO was unquestionable. When Sadat made his journey to Jerusalem, the Patriotic Coalition was the only party in Egypt which openly opposed his move and rightly predicted the inevitable deterioration of Arab solidarity and the consolidation of Israel's intransigent position.[8]

However, the voice of the Egyptian left was drowned in a sea of government propaganda. The leading daily *al-Ahram* rejected the publication of an article written by the distinguished Egyptian journalist Ahmed Baha El-Din. The article mildly warned the Egyptian writers not to be blindly carried away by the support for their government's position. Baha El-Din urged his colleagues to distinguish between the transitory relations between governments and the more lasting links between the Arab peoples. He added that while Egypt ought to be concerned with the events that were taking place in the Horn of Africa, yet it should not alienate itself from what was happening east of Sinai.[9]

To a large extent, the new Egyptian bourgeoisie managed to effect a major change in Egypt's political and economic disposition. Egypt changed its super-power patron and accordingly rearranged its alliances in the region and took a compromising attitude towards Israel. Internally, Sadat's regime favoured the flow of foreign capital into the country and left the task of economic development to the initiative of the growing private sector. The process of political liberalisation mainly benefited the politically active segments of the local bourgeoisie and undermined the position of the working classes and the trade unions. At the regional level, the Egyptian regime gradually dissociated itself from Arabism and the PRM and accepted a new role in Africa. Sadat's initiative was looked upon by the Western governments and the press as a step towards the realisation of peace in the Middle East. However, in reality it brought about the isolation of Egypt from the Arab East and created a deep rift between the people of Egypt and the rest of the Arabs.

On the other hand, the declared objectives of the visit which might be summed up in an Israeli withdrawal from the Arab territories occupied in 1967, and the establishment of a Palestinian entity were rapidly dashed by Israel's intransigence. Begin's willingness to compromise on even the minor issues such as the Israeli colonies in Sinai proved to be wanting.

As the dust of the journey to Jerusalem settled down, the worst fears of the Arabs were confirmed. Despite the exchange of courtesies, visits and even gifts, no substantial advance towards peace was achieved.

On the contrary, Israel chose to exploit the so-called 'historical event' to harden its old convictions; convictions that so long as Israel continued to say no to the Arabs, the Arabs would eventually accept the Zionist conditions for peace even if these conditions were modified every now and then. With this in mind, Begin proceeded in March 1978 to argue that the West Bank, which he regarded as Jewish soil by ancient right, was excluded from the UN Resolution 242 which called on Israel to withdraw from the occupied lands.

If Sadat meant his trip to be a shock treatment in the course of moving the peace process in the Middle East a step forward, Begin's response in the opposite direction had been more shocking. The unfortunate thing was that the USA had provided the latter with the adequate weaponry to sustain his irreconcilable stand. Perhaps no one knew better than Sadat that with Israel's response his peace efforts had run aground. In a speech delivered to the members of the People's Assembly before his last visit to the USA in February 1978, he made it clear to his audience that his initiative now belonged to the world at large and to history. Spelled out more accurately, he seemed to admit that his mission had failed in all but one respect, the dissociation of Egypt from the problems of the Arab East.

The reactions of all the factions of the PRM and some of the Arab regimes, especially Syria, Algeria, Iraq and South Yemen, better known as the Rejection Front, had been violently against Sadat. Iraq opted out of the new front and claimed it did so because the rejectionists were not ready to impose the severest measures against Egypt. Iraq also accused Syria of being unwilling to repudiate any solution of the Arab-Israeli conflict based on the UN Resolution 242. In reality, however, Iraq feared the unleashing of a new Kurdish rebellion on its northern borders if the Shah of Iran, encouraged by the USA, wished to do so. It would not be an exaggeration to say that perhaps such pressure had been exerted on Iraq to prevent its joining the Front. Therefore, by adopting a maximalist position, Iraq managed to get itself out of the new political game in the Middle East without much embarrassment.

The difference between Sadat and the Rejectionists, with the exception of the PLO, was not one between those who favoured a military solution and Egypt which opted for peace. Neither party was capable, willing or ready to launch a war against Israel. There was no doubt that all the Arab regimes had chosen a political settlement since the Khartoum Arab Summit in 1967. The October war in 1973 had the limited objective of putting the issue on the American agenda after a period of neglect. The Arab regimes did not perceive war as a substitute to a negotiated settlement. It was indicative in this respect to see how the Syrian forces in Lebanon refrained from intercepting the military action of the Israelis in southern Lebanon. Assad explained his inaction on that occasion as his permanent wisdom in not being dragged into a military confrontation with Israel at an inappropriate time and in the wrong place. As a rejectionist, he failed to achieve his declared aim for which he had occupied Lebanon, namely, the protection of the Palestinian Revolution and the preservation of Lebanese territorial sovereignty.

The rejectionists' main objection to Sadat's initiative stemmed from the conviction that apart from the utility of the move, it surrendered much to Israel without any compensation and drew Egypt away from the conflict in the region. Left on their own, the Syrians felt that their bargaining position *vis-à-vis* Israel had been weakened. Assad claimed that, 'Sadat helped make Israel stronger by neutralizing Egypt militarily'.[10] The only line of action which remained for the Rejection Front, perhaps better called the Objection Front, was to draw closer to the Soviet Union, exert pressure on Sadat in the hope of bringing Egypt back to the Arab fold, and avoid a military confrontation with Israel, even at the cost of losing face and more Arab territory.

On the other hand, Sadat's determination to steer away from any further entanglement with the problems of his Arab brethren might in time drive him to accept a bilateral agreement based on the economized generosity of Begin. According to the Time correspondent in Cairo: 'The likelihood is that he would go ahead and make his settlement with Israel, leaving those blank spaces on the treaty for the others to sign . . . .'[11] If not, Sadat's unlikely choice would be to attend a Saudi-sponsored Arab summit to iron out his differences with the other Arab leaders. In either case, the Palestinian question would be sacrificed on the altar of Arab solidarity and brotherhood, or permanent peace in the Middle East.

May 1978

Notes

1. *Newsweek*, 27 February 1978.
2. *Time*, 6 March 1978.
3. Ibid.
4. *Al-Ahram*, 20 December 1977.
5. Ibid., 3 March 1978.
6. Ibid., 9 December 1977.
7. Ibid., 8 December 1977.
8. See extracts from the statement issued by the Patriotic Coalition published in the monthly *Siyasa Duwaliyya*, Cairo, January 1978.
9. *Al-Ahali*, 22 March 1978.
10. *Newsweek*, 27 March 1978.
11. *Time*, 27 March 1978.

INDEX

Abdullah, King of Jordan 93
Africa 96-7, 100
al-Ahram 101, 105
al-Azm, Sadeq 72
al-Hakim, Tawfiq 103
al-Khatib, Ahmad 52-4
al-Nabar 41-2
Arab-Israeli conflict 16-17, 23-24,
    78-82, 84, 93-5, 101
Arabs: and June war 23-8; and
    Lebanese civil war 57-8; and
    October war 28-34; and
    Palestine 15-16; and PRM 35-8;
    and Palestinians 16, 17, 53,
    57-8, 67-8, 73-5, 84, 98-102;
    and USA 70-2; conditions in
    Arab countries 37-8, 41-3, 45-6,
    49, 68-70, 75-7, 81, 82, 83-5,
    87-92; increased solidarity of
    67-9; military strength of 23, 30;
    oppression in Arab countries
    69-70, 73, 89-90
Arafat, Yasir 32, 52, 54, 74
Assad, Hafez 17, 56, 57, 74, 77, 80,
    99, 107
Awad, Louis 103-4

Baath party 37, 46, 47-8, 99
Baha El-Din, Ahmed 105
Bank Misr 93-4
Begin, Menachem 78, 79, 87, 105,
    106, 107
bourgeoisie, petty 24, 31, 72
Brezhnev, Leonid Ilyich 60

censorship 69, 90, 99-100
conditions: in Arab countries 37-8,
    41-3, 45-6, 49, 68-70, 75-7,
    81, 82, 83-5, 87-92; in Egypt
    83, 84-5, 87-90, 91-2; in Lebanon
    41-3, 45-6

economy: of Egypt 93-4, 95-6; of
    Lebanon 40
Egypt 28, 29, 31, 33, 35, 53, 55, 57,
    58, 60, 67, 68, 75, 80, 81; and

Africa 96-7, 100; and October
    war 30; and other Arab countries
    96, 97-8, 102-3, 105, 106-7;
    and Palestinians 98, 99-102;
    and Russians 89, 92; and USA
    96-7; conditions in 83, 84-5,
    87-90, 91-2; economy of 93-4,
    95-6; food riots in 75-6, 89-90;
    parties in 104-5; peace initiative
    of 87-107; regime in 87-9
el-Siba'i, Youssef 101-2

Farouk, King of Egypt 93
Fateh 15, 24, 32, 35, 48, 51, 54, 99
Financial Times 54
Ford, President 59
Franjieh, Suleiman 44, 49, 53, 61

Gadhafi, Mu'ammer 31-2, 84
Geneva Conference 63, 64, 72, 74,
    85

Hassan, King of Morocco 95
Hourani, Albert 50
Hussein, King of Jordan, 35, 56, 57,
    74, 99
Hussein, Sharif 15

ideologies in Arab world: and June
    war 23-8; and October war
    28-34; formation of 21;
    'moderate' 25-6; 'modernist'
    27-8, 33-4; of PRM 21-2, 24-5,
    31-2, 35-6, 37, 38, 72-3;
    religious 26-7, 32-3
Idriss, Yousif 103
Iran 90, 96, 106
Iraq 32, 53, 58, 68, 74, 80, 82, 106
Israel 61, 67, 72, 81, 82, 96, 102;
    and Egyptian economy 94, 95-6;
    and Palestinians 79-80; and
    partitioning of Lebanon 55;
    and USA 71, 78-80; bargaining
    position of 30, 31, 78, 105-6;
    military strength of 28, 30,
    78-9, 92; public opinion in 95;

109